Souls Revealed

W9-AUK-528

Also by Dawn Marie Daniels and Candace Sandy

Souls of My Sisters

Souls of My Brothers

How Long Will They Mourn Me?

Souls Revealed.

*A Souls of My Sisters Book of
Revelations and Tools for Healing
Your Life, Soul, and Spirit*

WRITTEN AND EDITED BY
DAWN MARIE DANIELS
AND **CANDACE SANDY**

FOREWORD BY STAR JONES

SOULS OF MY SISTERS BOOKS
Kensington Publishing Corp.
http://www.kensingtonbooks.com

SOULS OF MY SISTERS books are published by

Kensington Publishing Corp. and Souls of My Sisters, Inc.
850 Third Avenue
New York, NY 10022

ISBN-13: 978-0-7582-2705-8
ISBN-10: 0-7582-2705-1

First Trade Paperback Printing: February 2008
10   9   8   7   6   5   4   3

Printed in the United States of America

Dedicated to

God and our mothers:

Ronnette Alvarez

Margaret Goerke

Patricia Samuel

Geraldine Hamlet

Helen Hamlet

Acknowledgments

Laurie Parkin, we thank you for believing in us. Steven and Walter Zacharius, your support is just amazing. Thank you, Jessica McLean Ricketts, for your advice and kindness. Thank you to Rakia Clark, John Scognamiglio, Kate Duffy, David Lappin, Valeece Smith, Adeola P. Saul, Magee King, Lydia Stein, Barbara Bennett, Esq., Selena James, Mercedes Fernandez, Neven Gravett, and Daly Hernandez. Thank you, Karen Thomas, for the beginning of the dream.

Our thanks to all the women of *Souls of My Sisters* and *Souls Revealed*. We appreciate the team of individuals who have given their hearts and souls to help us develop, edit, and create the concepts, ideas, and thoughts within these pages: Dr. Jarralynne Agee, for her remarkable ability to provide focus, content, and themes; Chandra Spark Taylor, who edited numerous drafts and constantly encouraged us; our general counsel Kojo Bentil, Esq., Ann Brown, Dr. Elisabeth Jackson-English, our editorial assistant, Prince Michael Vincent, and Vernell Campbell for their dedication. Tamika and Bobby Quillard of Quillard Inc. for their cover artwork and logo design. Nicole Wild and the Women's Alliance/Chapter 2 in Miami. Lastly, Linda Peterson and Peterson Harley for their support.

Special Thanks From Candace Sandy

To my parents, Patricia and Carlton Samuel, who love with grace and have instilled in me the need to make a difference. To my brothers, Sherwin Sandy and Sheldon Samuel, my nieces, Crystal and Taylor, and nephew, Ricardo, who have always been supportive. To my aunts for their undying love, belief, guidance, and support: Geraldine (Amu), Helen, Jennifer, Hemetta, Joanie, Pat, and Joan Braithwaite. To my uncles, who are absolutely phenomenal: Vernell (Vush) and Trevor Hamlett and Wendell Hamlet, who never stopped believing in us. To my cousins, whose love sustains me: Jackie, Ann, Paula, Torrie, Jodelle, Donica, Danica, and Natalie. To all of the boys I treasure: Kealon, Terrence, Mark, Trevon, Brent, Franklin, Elijah Langston. To the Fraley family, my aunt and uncle, Frank and Lisa Fraley, and to Aunt Ollie Gables and Grandmother Fraley. To my godmother, Cyrilla Laborde, and my extended family: Gary and Amy Krakow, Saundra Parks, and my godchildren, Mark, Martin, Chanel, Naomi, Eliana, and Alyssa. To Cristina Colon and Maggie Goring, my sisters since I was nine years old, and their spouses,

Jose Gerrero and James Goring. To Al and Tiffany Ragin, who are simply irreplaceable.

To Calvin Nelson and Curtis Taylor for dreaming a bigger dream for us, and Dr. Arek Jahimovich. To Congressman Gregory W. Meeks, his wife, Simone Marie Meeks, the Washington and New York staffs, who have been encouraging and understanding during the development of the book. Special thanks to Alithia Alleyne, J. C. Callender, Rachia Hazel, Carl E. Simmons, Ricardo Dorcean, Dr. Elisabeth Jackson-English, Terry English, Doris Jennings, Nadia Suliaman, the Donna Karan family, and Vera Gaskin. Also to Brenda Moore and Congresswomen Gwen Moore, photographers Margot Jordan, Nat Valentine, and Ronnie Wright, One Wheels, Inc., Karen and Randi Payton, Tonya Payton, Elisa Grubb, Dirty Genius Co., and Marion Brown. Thanks to all of the women in *Souls Revealed* for their candor and honesty, and to Donna Wilson and Cherryl Brownley.

Special Thanks From Dawn Marie Daniels

To my very special mirrors, Mark and Martin. You show me my true self every day. Your love and support, questions and answers, laughter and tears have taught me the best lessons I have learned in life. You are truly special sons.

Sincere love and undying devotion to my best friend and sister, Candace Sandy. Your unconditional love and support have sustained me for the last fifteen years of my life—you are truly my hero. Your love and compassion inspires me to be the best person I can be every day.

To some of my dear friends, Christine Saunders, Tiffany Cordy, Laura Santiago, Melody Guy, Joella Irving, Lavonne Hall, Lorna Lightfoot, and Antoinette Callistro. Thank you for being my every day cheering squad. I appreciate your sisterly advice and support.

Mom, the love you have shown me and the lessons you have taught me will remain with me forever. I love you and pray for you every day! Only a really special dad would drop whatever he was doing on the other side of the country to support his daughter's dream. Daddy, you are that special person and I cannot express in words how much I love you.

Thank you Grandma, you are truly an angel. You are always there to support anything I do and I am grateful for the love and joy you bring to my life.

To the future, my little niece, Mimi. Auntie loves you and knows you are destined for greatness!

My sister, Kim, you are so wise for your age! You keep me focused and on point and for that I love you. Alicia, I love you and pray for you every day. To my brothers, Danny, Darryl, and David. Although we are miles away from each other, I love you and think of you every day.

Contents

Foreword

The Reinvention of You!

Star Jones

The Lord shall preserve you from all evil:
he shall preserve your soul.
The Lord shall preserve your going out
and your coming in from this time forth,
and even forevermore.
—Psalms 121

I had become intoxicated with my own life. When I began my career working for the Brooklyn District Attorney's office as a prosecutor, I absolutely loved what I did. The feelings and emotions evoked by the privilege of using the words "Star Jones on behalf of the People of New York" inside a courtroom has never been replicated by anything I have done in the world of journalism or entertainment; yet, somehow I knew God had more in store for me, and the desire to discover it overwhelmed me like an all-encompassing flame. My job title and physical location never defined me, and my drive and passion for the life I always saw for myself were great motivations. I worked tirelessly and with each turn there were blessings beyond my own expectations. As the Bible says, "To whom much is given, even more is expected." But over time, I extended myself too far and started playing a "role" instead of being a person, and I stifled my own desires to appease other people. In the process, I lost my genuine connection with myself and the audience who'd made me a household name.

I take one hundred percent responsibility for enjoying my celebrity too much. My life seemed perfect, didn't it? I enjoyed planning the wedding of my dreams and marrying the man I had always hoped to share my life with. I was featured in magazines and on red carpets galore. I had a great job. But still, I wasn't living to my highest standards. My values were being compromised every single day. I felt enormous guilt and shame about not going public about the state of my health. I honestly felt that since it was *my* health, I had to deal with it in a private, personal way. I knew there would be backlash, but I needed time to process my emotions and the hardnosed truth that my obesity had reached such a critical stage that I required surgery to even begin to get a handle on it. I just wasn't ready to publicly open the floodgates to the pain I had tucked inside.

I was afraid—like maybe you are, too. Plain and simple, I screwed up! But I've learned that you can't let fear keep you from doing the things you know you should be doing.

The recent events in my public life have given me the opportunity to check myself, so to speak. And after straying off course, I am using my experience to empower other women.

With God as my source and with a redefined mission for my life, I recognize that, in His eyes, I am capable and acceptable as is. I let Him lead my passions and purpose, and I simply put them into action. I have learned not to run from myself or from any crisis put before me. Instead, I stand fast and really look at what God is trying to tell me. I have so much more that I am able to give, and I know that you do, too.

Is there room for you to make a comeback in your own life? God says yes! The first thing to do is forgive. I needed to forgive *myself,* and maybe you do, too. Forgiveness is the key to letting you utilize your life for what it is supposed to be. You don't want that part of yourself muddied up with long-simmering toxic problems. Figure out how to get past these things. When I began the process of forgiveness, I freed myself; and "when the Lord makes you free . . . you are freed indeed."

For a while, I diverted my attention away from what was truly important. So if you can take anything from my experience, take this: don't get sidetracked by limiting yourself, or worse, letting other people put limitations on you. You are the *editor* of the only dictionary that defines you.

This is where *Souls Revealed* can offer guidance.

Whether you are exploring your Hold Back Factor, weathering a storm while Standing in the Gap of Grace, managing The Process of Self-Love, or struggling in Life Support, other women have been there, too. The women of *Souls Revealed* will happily equip you with the tools—based on their own personal experiences—to plan your ultimate comeback. We know all too well that the pain that happens to one woman has a ripple effect for us all. Together, we can prepare to be put on the path to a fulfilling, purposeful and beautiful life.

Star Jones, a former prosecutor and best-selling author, is best known for her candor, confidence, and legal expertise on television. She has received critical acclaim as a news and legal correspondent, and in 2007, was named the executive editorial producer and host of *Star Jones,* her own "Tru TV" daytime talk show. After her initial debut on "Tru TV" in 1991, Jones became the legal correspondent for NBC; hosted her own syndicated talk show, *Jones & Jury;* was senior correspondent and chief legal analyst for *Inside Edition;* hosted *Live from the Red Carpet* for *E!* "Entertainment Television;" and was a co-host of the Emmy®-winning talk show *The View* for nine years.

Introduction

When we first published Souls of My Sisters we didn't know what to expect. We were focused on helping women of color heal by sharing their experiences with others. We were amazed at the responses we received as we spoke across the country to tens of thousands of women. So many women were in pain and didn't know how to deal with the issues they were facing. Whether it was an abusive spouse, a disobedient child, an ailing parent, or a dissatisfying job experience, they all felt alone. When women of Souls of My Sisters spoke about the things they faced and how free they felt to tell their stories, we saw so many lightbulbs brighten over the heads in the audience. Whether it was because of the nods of agreement or the cries of, "Say that again, sister, for the cheap seats!," we knew something was happening, but we weren't quite sure what it was at the time.

While we included "Your Personal Book of Revelations" in *Souls of My Sisters,* we didn't realize just how important revelations are to our individual lives. Oprah calls revelations epiphanies, "those aha moments" when everything makes perfect sense. Things that didn't make sense before just appear to fall into place as though it was that way all the while, but we just realized it for the first time. We thought hard about this for a long time. What makes those epiphanies possible? How can we get to them sooner without having to suffer through the drama, self-inflicted or not?

Souls Revealed will help you take the responsibility for healing your own life. We want to share all that we've learned because we believe, as women of color, we are truly the experts of our lives and cultural experience. Who knows better than we do how we feel about issues concerning our lives? We're not saying that we don't believe in theology, psychology, or sociology; what we're saying is no one knows you better than you and your sisters who have experienced the same thing.

How good do you feel when you have achieved a goal? Do you want to pump your fist in the air and shout, "I did it!"? We have found that when we have a revelation that makes us feel as if we have just solved an ancient mystery, everything seems to be so clear. It is like you have just won the cosmic lottery. If you were stuck, you immediately become unstuck and mobilize your spirit into action.

As women of color, we, like anyone else, seek happiness and satisfaction in order to fulfill our need for security, joy, and belonging. But as women, we try to live up to what we believe others perceive. There are so many ways we block those feelings because we are so busy pleasing others. And we wonder why we're treated like doormats when we lie down on the ground so everyone else can have clean feet? It doesn't matter if you are in a corporate setting or sitting at home or in a car on the street, society has a perception of you.

But what if it isn't you? What if you're not the go-to person for everything in your family? What if you just want to live your life? What if you are "baby momma" number three, have three children and a high school diploma, but you want to be a doctor or a lawyer? When and how do you come to realize that anything is possible?

"When you give yourself permission to be human," says Harvard's How to Be Happy course instructor and psychologist Tal Ben-Shahar, "you are more likely to open yourself up to positive emotions." It's time for us to think positively about who we are and not let society dictate who we should be. We've been stereotyped as angry black women who can't keep a man. And the sad part about it is that, over time, we have come to believe what has been said about us.

We want change and we want it now. Realizing what is good for us and what we need to do to get there is the process of revelation. How can we achieve that before we find ourselves in situations that bring us down? How can we say, "Wait a minute—I'm not getting caught up in this mess!"

We totally believe in the power of positive thinking, but how do you get to the positive thought—or should we say the healthy thought?—before you've gone down the wrong road? The path isn't the problem—it's how we use the process to get to the realization that change needs to take place in ourselves. We have made plenty of mistakes, but it is the lessons we've learned that have made us stronger, wiser, and more grateful for all God has done for us.

Are you on life support? What we mean by this is, are you just barely existing, unable to deal with the multitude of issues coming at you on a daily basis. We know that sometimes we feel as if we are in a batting cage with no helmet and a little plastic bat, and balls are being propelled at us a mile a minute and all we can do is manage to hit as many as we can and dodge the rest. We have a friend, Tammy, who we know is on life support. She's great at her high-pressure job, has a loving and supportive family and a boyfriend who's helpful, but she's a basket case. Tammy has found herself involuntarily shaking in a corner, unable to move due to panic attacks.

Here is a woman who has the respect of her industry, everything that many women wish they had, but is unable to cope with the simple mundane tasks that are a part of life.

Everything spiraled out of control so much that she went to her doctor to get a prescription for antidepressants. On the outside looking in, anyone would say she lives a charmed life, but she feels as if she is a prisoner in her own body.

So many of us are on life support with only a thread holding it all together. If you are not on life support, we are sure that you know someone who is. It may not be as drastic as it sounds, but clarity comes with exploration. Our goal is that this book will act as a conduit to your consciousness that houses your innermost feelings. Many of the women in *Souls of My Sisters* were brave enough to tell their stories and have found tremendous healing in the process.

Maria Davis, who was dealing with the fact that she had full-blown AIDS when we asked her to tell her story, had such a spiritual awakening and healing through the release of her personal testimony.

At first she was resistant to letting her family, friends, and colleagues know she had the AIDS virus. "Are you crazy?" was her response when we asked her to tell her story. It wasn't until after we coaxed and guided her to tell her story that her true purpose was revealed.

Her realization has not only saved her life, even though doctors had told her she didn't have long to live, but it has saved thousands of lives because she was willing to shout from the rooftops that she has AIDS and you can get it, too, if you're not careful.

Who would have known that her purpose in life would be the healing of others, but it did. That's how powerful a revelation truly is. In theological terms a revelation is God's disclosure of Himself and His will to His creatures. We all know how powerful that is for us all. Why is it that we don't think of our own personal revelations as having the same power? A revelation can change the course of the world.

Are you accepting of fractional ownership? There is a popular trend which has created a new consumer breed called "transumers" or "fractional owners." Fractional owners may find it difficult to save up and care for a particular item and/or property.

Instead of becoming the sole owner of the property, you purchase a share of it, as do fifteen other people. It's less risky, as you own $\frac{1}{15}$ of the property and have others to share in the burden of maintenance and taxes. This may be a good choice for individuals who want to be cautious in their spending and avoid sole financial responsibility for big-ticket items like vacation homes, jets, yachts, and exotic cars. Without the expense that full ownership entails, they can focus instead on the experience those goods can provide.

But are you choosing fractional ownership when it comes to your beliefs and values? Do you seek to share the responsibility of your feelings, experiences, and circumstances rather than fully commit and take ownership of your stuff?

To lessen the burden we find ourselves agreeing to let someone else manage our most valuable asset, our soul, and let them utilize it and then pass it along to someone else when they are done for a fraction of the price. We do it every day by allowing partners to come in and out of our lives like a revolving door, or worse, by committing to someone who is in a relationship but wants to enjoy all that we have to offer. Then there are parents who are not committed to caring for their children and leave the rearing to other people and/or relatives.

Step-parenting can be rewarding if you are committed to raising a child because of your love for their parent. But there are times that it can be painful when your partner allows and accepts fractional ownership. We were told a story about a stepfather who helped raise his wife's two children and happily paid for college. It was time for his oldest stepdaughter to get married and again he lovingly footed the bill for the wedding. The daughter wanted her biological father, who had never been around physically or helped support her, to walk her down the aisle.

It had been her dream ever since she was a little girl and her mother agreed. When the wife presented the idea to her husband he became angry—after all, he was the one fully committed each and every day, never missing any of her after-school activities and sharing in the responsibility. He insisted that he deserved to walk her down the aisle.

The husband and wife squared off; according to the wife, how could she prevent her daughter from wanting her birth father to walk her down the aisle? The stepfather was eventually granted his wish, but it caused such resentment and anger that it became the catalyst for the eventual divorce of the parents.

Your life and experience are not for rent or sale, they do not belong in the bargain bin amongst last season's collection. Living for less diminishes our soul and causes a rupture in our authentic self. As African-American women we have to say *no more* to bargaining with our souls! Collectively, if we live for less and accept that we have been messed up and over used and thrown away, stabbed in the back, or choose not to speak out when we are demeaned, we will offer our lives at a fraction of the cost which will only lessen our legacy, creating a disservice and an infraction on the generations that come after us.

Souls Revealed invites you to move out of toxic relationships, move yourself from despair, depression, and hopelessness into a place where you can be truthful, loving, and accepting of yourself for your gifts and shortcomings, and most of all, take responsibility for your actions.

Within these pages and online at *www.soulsofmysisters. com,* you can explore some of the experiences and processes that are part of the lives of black women. Regardless of where you are, we want to be a part of your greater revelation concerning women of color. We want to show how you, too, can take part in that powerful journey. As women of color, we have an awesome power and an even greater responsibility to share our gifts with each other.

How to Use This Book

As with any communication, read this book with an open mind. As you learn about other people's experiences and observe their journey to personal revelation, reserve judgment. It is so easy to say, "That could never be me." We never know how we will react in a crisis. When tragedy occurs, black women's stress responses often are "tend, befriend, mend, and keep it in," according to Dr. Angela Neal-Barnett, an award-winning psychologist. "Rather than being seen as less than she is supposed to be, a strong black woman refuses to admit she is stressed and keeps her feelings and emotions bottled up inside while she helps everyone else. This strategy makes the black woman an excellent candidate for the development of anxiety."

So many of us give so much to others, we no longer have anything to sustain ourselves, creating a climate for depression, victim mentality, and anxiety attacks. We become weak, clinging to things that make us feel good—food, shopping, alcohol, sex—anything to numb the emptiness and pain.

We learned so many valuable lessons, but we recognized that even with knowledge in our own personal lives there is a process that we all must go through if we want to begin to deal successfully with our issues.

As you grow and become more spiritually aware, your life

expands—the challenges become greater and the accountability increases.

You can't hide behind *I didn't know* or *if I knew*. It becomes increasingly more difficult for someone to pull the wool over your eyes. They say, "God blesses fools and babies," but you are neither and you know when you are being duped. It makes you uneasy when you are in the presence of a fair-weather friend; it's just not right to have a man anymore just for the sake of saying you have one. You are ready to give your very best and commit to the relationship, family, and your life's purpose, but when he is not equally committed to truth, love, generosity, growth, and partnership with you in spirit and responsibility, you no longer have space for him in your life.

We say it's you who doesn't fit in, because your partner will always be who he is; he will change in his own time and season, or maybe not, but it's you who have changed.

It may make you restless if you find yourself, regardless of your accomplishments, putting your life on hold. There is fear instilled due to emotional disappointment. Opportunities may have been thrown away, or we have suffered abuse from life and love, plus loss of fortunes and close relationships.

The residue of the pain remains prominent—how do you get past this? By being in the middle—self-awareness and open to transformation.

We are here to remind you that in the middle of all the painful mess there still lies a beautiful woman who is, in spite of the restrictions and circumstances, worthy of compassion and forgiveness. We are your support system for your journey, no matter how painful it may become. Always know that you are never alone.

In each chapter we ask soul revealing questions and offer tips that you can use to begin your personal revelation process, no matter what problems you are facing. It is important to be an active participant in your own healing. You can read the words, but if you don't reveal your thoughts there is nothing we or anyone else can do to help you discover you. You are the author of your own story, and believe us, it is a best-seller. This book will help you to construct your all-important innermost thoughts.

Your answers to the questions and your thought process throughout the exercises will act as conduits to your subconscious. We don't have the answers to your problems—they are buried deep inside of you. The brief glimpses into the lives of the women who have shared their stories in *Souls of My Sisters* and *Souls Revealed* provide a guide to finding inspiration and a new way to approach your own life. You will be asked to share your innermost thoughts and that will lead you on an introspective journey.

Each chapter ends with a thought or biblical quote that we call Revelations Revealed. We also incorporate a key you can use in your own life, ultimately bringing you closer to the divine truth buried inside you. We ask you to write your thoughts in Your Revelations Revealed.

Souls Revealed seeks to assist black women to rid themselves of self-judgment and shame. Together we strive for collective healing, to learn from our stories so we can enjoy our triumphs and face our challenges.

You may not read the book from cover to cover—regardless of the part of the process that you may be in, keep it with you. When you are comfortable and ready to work through the truth of your own life, your sisters will be waiting.

Souls Revealed

CHAPTER 1

Life Support

Most of the major roadblocks in our lives are not tests from God, but are self-inflicted. We go in circles, avoiding our purpose, not making decisions, sabotaging ourselves, and basically barely holding our lives together.

You may know life support as medical terminology to describe a state when individual body systems can no longer function efficiently. In order to sustain the body, an artificial means is used to stabilize and prolong one's life. Your breathing may need the assistance of a mechanical ventilator; tubes hooked up to machines become a lifeline for your vital organs. You lie in a comatose state and aren't able to make decisions for yourself so that power has been relegated to your spouse or health proxy. Without directives or clear instructions your loved ones are left to make decisions about your life. Publicly they will quantify each decision as being what you would have wanted. Actually, these decisions are based on their own abilities, needs, and convenience.

The thought of leaving decisions about your life in someone else's hands is very scary. We can all think of a few people in our lives whom we would not want to have this responsibility without clear directives.

How about not leaving the decisions to anyone? Many of us go through life just existing, too frightened to make decisions, leaving everything to chance. They are the people who tell you, "I don't know. It just happened." You may be that person or have felt that way. You check out of life for a period of time when you just can't do anything but exist. We've all experienced that state. Life support has kicked in—life continues, you are not really living.

The concept of life support is clear. We are waiting for someone to save us, when we know deep in our hearts that we have to save ourselves. And that doesn't start with a visit to the doctor's office—it starts with a trip through our own minds. By challenging our own thoughts we can create new patterns of behavior, happiness, and success. Many books encourage us to think happy thoughts, look on the bright side, and change the way we view our lives. That's easier said than done, but how do you do it? How do you make sustainable change in your life? First, by recognizing that it is your responsibility to do it. There are a lot of things that we should do for ourselves but we have found ways to get other people to help us. If we are too busy and too stressed, others can come and clean our homes. If we aren't able, someone else can feed our families. Even if we don't make the changes necessary to rid ourselves of that baby fat, we can raise enough money to get liposuction. Others can work in our homes, change our bodies, and help us get new jobs. But no one has found a way to change our minds for us.

This is a crucial lesson. The way we think dictates the way we behave and respond. In fact, if we go into a situation believing that something is not good, we will automatically seek out those experiences that confirm the negative status of that endeavor. Conversely, if we want to believe something is good, we seek out evidence to prove that fact. If you aren't sure of this, think of any situation that someone accused a child that you loved of doing something wrong. You think of every reason that they could be wrong. You wanted to hold that innocent opinion of the child. Now, why don't we give ourselves the same courtesy, to believe and expect the best about ourselves?

The "At Least" Factor

Some of us are just holding on as if life is happening around you but you can't actively participate because YOU are holding you back. Being in a state of life support is what we call the "at least" factor. The *Oxford Dictionary* defines the word *least* as the smallest in the amount of degree; lowest in importance.

It's a lessening of who we are as women—by staying in a marriage where your husband has not lived with you for years because you tell yourself at least you are still legally married; remaining in a job where you are mistreated or underpaid because at least you have a job; getting involved in a marriage or relationship that you know is unhealthy and worse staying in a marriage or relationship that is stressful and toxic; loving someone who is emotionally unavailable; overeating or starving yourself; raising children who are not responsible because their father is not around; being in denial about a sick child; waiting to the last possible minute to do anything; battling a disease by yourself; dealing with aging parents and siblings who are not doing their own share; having a closet full of clothes and no significant savings; competing at your workplace or with your mate; or maintaining friendships with people who have toxic personalities because at least you won't be alone. Whether it involves addiction, finances, family, or co-dependency, you deserve to let God give you more.

As parents we get really annoyed when our children tell us, at least they're not on the street selling drugs when they don't bring home the A's that are expected of them. Our response to them, as it would be to anyone else, is why would you expect so little of yourself? Aspirations are not about seeking downward but looking higher and beyond one's current state. It has become too commonplace for us to say, "At least I _____." You fill in the blank. What gets us to this point at such a young age? When did it become so commonplace to settle for less? That's not what our ancestors believed in because if it was, we wouldn't be here today.

The "at least" factor is any woman's propensity to minimize the negative issues in her life in order to justify her current situation. To believe you should get more than you have been getting, you should expect more than you have been receiving.

To put the "at least" factor to the true test, try any one of the following statements and see how they sound to you.

At least I got a job.

At least my boss doesn't treat me as bad as he did my predecessor.

At least I got a man.

At least he comes home to me when he's done.

At least my credit is good enough for this kind of car.

At least my child straightens up when his daddy is around.

At least I'm not as heavy as my girlfriend.

Some part of you read this and didn't like the way "at least" sounds. At first glance these statements are limiting and depressing. It is not encouraging to think of how we compromise about some of the most important things in our lives. But, take another look at each of these statements and see how you would feel if these words were spoken by Oprah Winfrey or freedom fighter Sojourner Truth or the pastor at your church. What do you think would have become of Oprah if she had settled for less? How far do you think any of the slaves would have gone if Sojourner Truth had settled for a plantation that "at least" wasn't as bad as the other one? What if she had accepted ("anywhere but here") instead of going all the way to freedom? What if your pastor said, "We are going all the way to heaven and sit on the steps of the pearly gates." You would want to go in those pearly gates, so what kind of person would you have to be to make it all the way?

There's not a mystical or magical plan that makes some women sit at the steps of the gates and others walk on in. There are circumstances of our birth that make some goals a longer shot for some women than others, but God gave us all the right and the opportunity to choose.

In the most practical terms, what if we were to give you a camera that only had a lens pointed toward the ground? You would think the world was a dirty, uninteresting place. If you focus on the least, you block what you have coming to you. So instead, focus on the most optimal place that you can imagine. The disadvantage of dreaming big is the possibility of a major disappointment if you fail. The advantage is the amazing feeling of victory if you succeed.

We will let you in on a little secret. We have interacted with so many people who are at the top of their games in politics, music, entertainment, and even sports, and we have found that successful people haven't just had everything handed to them. We wrote this book but you could write the next one. We know lots of writers and most of them have to work hard to complete the perfect manuscript that you buy. But the difference between these superstars and average women is they have high expectations and they move forward with each dream "as if."

"As if" they are the most talented people on their work teams.

"As if" the perfect men are just waiting to meet them.

"As if" the solution to their child's experience at school is building on what's right to overcome what might be wrong.

Exercise

Think of one of the most significant areas in your life that you would like to see change. You must be honest about your feelings and where you are at this stage of your life. Allow yourself to complete all of the "at least" statements that come to mind about your current situation and jot them down as a sentence. Write a statement about any area of your life:

Job and/or career	Love life
Marriage	Family roles
Your children's performance	Your health
Your weight	Your habits
Your finances today	Your future finances

Instructions:

1. Take the time to do that right now by spending at least five minutes going over the areas in your life that you could improve, then spend five minutes writing down all of your "at least" statements that make your current situation viable.

2. After you have written your list, go back and read through it again. See if you notice any patterns about things that are working for you and the areas where the "at least" factor is actually holding you back.

3. Use the following chapters to figure out what is keeping
    you from wanting, and expecting, the best from the life
    you have now.

When you settle for the least amount of anything, that is
exactly what you will get, so don't be surprised. We've met so
many women across the country who have shared with us
how their boyfriends or husbands have abused them and
when we ask them why they accept that type of treatment
their response is, "At least I have a man." Yes, you do and he
will literally love you to death if you let him.

In our society, less isn't more. Black women are designed
to achieve greatness. We should never settle for less, which is
what gets us to that point where we become dependent on life
support. We don't have to think outside the box or look for
anything better because we don't believe it exists. In part this
is because we are afraid of failing or being disappointed, hurt,
alone, abandoned, destitute, or even being successful. Fear is
a big part of why we get to being on life support. It paralyzes
the senses and puts us in a state of immobility.

How Do We Get to This Point?

There are many experiences in life that can make anyone
want to check out for a period of time. It can be an unexpected traumatic experience or the slow burn of stress. Whatever the cause, maybe it has to be dealt with in order to move
past the state of being socially, emotionally, and spiritually
comatose.

Take our friend Stacia,[*] for example. Stacia is a beautiful, successful, career-oriented woman. She owns her home and has a loving husband. Out of nowhere, Stacia developed panic attacks that left her emotionally and physically debilitated. Not sure of the cause, Stacia went to her doctor, who prescribed medication. When Stacia was asked how she felt, she said she was what she called "emotionally numb" and that left her feeling calm and panic-free. But when asked if she ever found out the cause of the panic attacks, she said no. How can something be fixed if you don't know what caused the problem in the first place?

Many of us sense or even know we have a problem, but instead of actually dealing with it we want to circumvent it. We want the quickest solution to a problem that may have taken years to manifest. Give us a pill for this or a shot for that, but we don't want to know exactly what is going on. We love Stacia and we are not against her using medication to help her cope with her attacks, but we want to know what it is that caused them so she can deal with that as well.

Many of us don't go to a doctor for medication to deal with our stressful situations. We use other forms of therapy instead. Retail therapy, sex therapy, alcohol therapy, and food therapy. None of us are immune and all of us indulge in something or other to bring us joy, but when we use these things as crutches they become a part of our life support network but don't necessarily help us deal with what got us there in the first place.

*Stacia is not her real name.

Do you have a pattern that keeps you on life support? We have a girlfriend who, whenever something bad happens, goes to the store and buys things for her house. You may say OK, that's not so bad. But she has nowhere to put these things or even the space to use them. She buys glasses, linens, lighting fixtures, candelabras, napkin rings and all the things people would use to entertain others, but has no use for these items in her already congested house because she never entertains there. You can't tell her she doesn't need these things because she just tells you she will use these for her house, all the while she stores them in a room that she could utilize as a dining room!

Meanwhile, she's a single mother of two struggling to make ends meet. We know she is depressed about her failed marriage and wishes things were different, but until she faces this fact she will remain in a state of life support—just existing for her children and going through the motions from day to day, and, oh yes, buying another set of wineglasses.

Running a High Fever

There are hundreds of thousands of black women who are running a high fever, which is one of the symptoms that can lead you to life support. Without any intervention, just a few more events can make their lives literally catastrophic. Those events can take the shape of people and things that prevent you from dealing with the truth about you.

Going through life with a high fever causes you to carry around issues that have occurred in the past, but were never resolved. Subconsciously it becomes almost an internal mantra, embedding itself as part of your value system. You will defend it at all costs. This will occupy your soul and shape all your patterns and practices. A slow burn can easily deplete your energy, hindering your ability to make good, soulful decisions.

Chlarissa Pope's Story

"My life was rocky at best. We went without electricity, water, and food quite often. There were times when I would beg from other kids at the lunch table, then put the food and milk they gave me in my backpack and bring them home. I was proud. I felt as though I was helping my mom take care of us. I was too young to understand that after carrying the milk in my backpack all day, it often spoiled. When I asked my mom where the milk went, she always told me she drank it so as not to dampen my spirit.

"Mom worked multiple jobs to make ends meet. She was so selfless that she sold her blood just to have enough money to buy food and other things we needed. Where was my dad, you may ask? Dad wasn't there because he didn't want to be. Dad was married, taking his new family to theme parks and appearing to be having a grand time. My mom tried as hard as she could to make up for all the shortcomings, but nothing can take the place of a father's love in a little girl's heart. I entered my teen years angry at my mom, my dad, and the world. I knew my mom loved me and did the best she could, but something was still missing and it made me angry. I began searching for something . . . someone to complete me. The next thing I knew, I was pregnant at seventeen.

"Someone said, 'I thought you were going to be something,' as if my having a child at seventeen automatically committed me to a life of failure. That statement fueled some-

thing monstrous within me. I was now considered a statistic, but I refused to BECOME A STATISTIC. I was determined not to disappoint my unborn son. My son wasn't going to have to struggle like I did. My son's father was handsome, sweet, and said all the right things, so I just knew he would be there for me. I was wrong. His love and sincerity went right out the window when I refused to have an abortion.

"I lived a life of single motherhood. I worked fifty-six or more hours a week. I went to school full time, cared for my son, cooked, cleaned the house, and started all over again the next week. At first, I was angry at his father and tried to make him do right by our son. I would lash out and make threats, but as time went on, I took that energy and transformed it into the fuel I needed to find my path to success.

"I went on to accomplish many things, including completing my master's degree while involved in many activities and organizations. My son, Ja'len, is extremely smart and handsome—we are very close. I had great friends but I still felt as though I wasn't doing enough. I began to fall into a depression, feeling as though I didn't deserve to be loved. I was always tired and just wanted to give up. Christ, Ja'len, and my mom are the reasons I didn't end up in a psych ward or dead. I was too embarrassed and proud to see a psychiatrist. I began ordering self-help books from the Internet in a frantic attempt to find answers to my problems."

Chlarissa was running a high fever for a very long time. She didn't realize how her father's abandonment and her son's father's abandonment had affected her. She continued doing all the things she felt needed to be done, but wasn't fulfilled. Outwardly, she was a loving and successful mom, a highly sought-after marketing consultant and beautiful sister to boot. Inside told a different story. Chlarissa was insecure and angry and didn't know where those feelings came from.

"I felt like I was losing control of my emotions . . . that is, until I read *Souls of My Sisters*." Chlarissa was able to see herself in the stories of other sisters and began the process of reducing her high fever. She decided to start the Souls of My Sisters Conference: Women in the Mirror, in Little Rock, AR. She wanted to share her experience and help other women as she'd been helped. The conference has grown from seventy-five to hundreds of women who attend events in several cities throughout the South and Midwest every year. Chlarissa was able to say, "No more to just existing, no more to life support." Black women are too good not to live lives of happiness and prosperity.

The Disease to Please

Very few of us practice preventative medicine of the body, so why would it be expected that we would practice preventative medicine of the mind, heart, or spirit? Many women of color are on the edge. We go through the motions because we are expected to and tend to neglect the most important person in our lives: ourselves. Believe it or not, we are trained from a very young age to sacrifice ourselves for the sake of our families and friends. We put everything in front of ourselves because we are told we are the only ones who can make things better, so we must compromise ourselves. It's not just what we hear from our families—it is what we hear from everyone. We are good enough to clean kitchens, feed presidents, raise dignitaries and socialites, run multimillion-dollar businesses, yet we are still degraded in public and constantly have to prove ourselves.

We are all guilty of spreading ourselves too thin and trying to please everyone, yet somehow we still expect our needs to be met. You may find yourself going above and beyond to prove you can work the hardest and longest—and best. Sometimes it's not solely our ambition that drives us, but our need and desire to please others. It is your way of proving that you are loyal and devoted. But none of that loyalty, devotion, or energy is being directed back into your own life. It has been ingrained in us that women of color should provide and support others before we focus on ourselves.

We have a wake-up call for you. That was then and this is now. Society evolves and so do the roles and lives of black women. More than ever, we are breaking our backs to make the lives of our friends, family, partners, children, and employers better, and we wonder why people are not grateful but just want more.

While they are constantly withdrawing from what they believe is an abundance of resources, no one is depositing back into our life account. We aren't demanding that the people around us put in their equal share. Instead we compensate for everyone's weakness because of our need to please others.

But at what price? Everything in life has a price. What are you willing to pay for the life you are currently living? Look around. Fifty percent of black women are heading their households. Many are single and/or divorced. Still more are suffering with depression. Numbers of black women will die this year alone of diabetes and heart attacks. We deny ourselves the abundance of love that God has for us and instead replace it with self-hatred. We condemn ourselves for the mistakes we make and for years refuse ourselves forgiveness. For many years Dawn condemned herself to being a bad wife. She married young and didn't understand why she couldn't save her husband from the path he chose. They had been high school sweethearts, but things changed and there was nothing she could do about it. Dawn blamed herself for many years about why things went so wrong. It was a journey she had to take on her own and it wasn't easy or pretty. She realized she couldn't make him happy or change how he felt about himself and he couldn't be the captain of her happiness either. Dawn's ex-husband and she are friends now, but it took a long road to get there.

We look to other people to create the illusion of a safe place, take on the relationship and get mad when the other person has had enough of us living off their soul. For example, how do you think you would feel if you were married to a people-pleaser who was pleasing everyone and looking to you to join in on the charade? Would you be happy and join in or say, oh no, not me, not anymore?

The Little Angry Capsule

We all have those deep, dark secrets we have kept from everyone because we refused to face the pain. The hurt that occurs at any age, if not dealt with, can keep you angry. It's like swallowing a time-release capsule: the effects of the pill come on in time and are released slowly until the medicine takes full effect. Pretty soon, before we know it, we become so happy to be angry, we even rehearse it.

Kenya is a very sweet person.* She's good at what she does and enjoys life to the fullest. It wasn't until Kenya got a new boss that she learned what anger could do to a person. Kenya's boss knew just how to push her buttons, and it wasn't just Kenya. She basically pushed everyone's buttons, but it was Kenya who internalized it the most. Kenya would seethe with anger just at the sound of her boss's voice. It was like chewing glass for her. At one point she became so angry she went to her boss's superior and asked to either be let go or given another position.

Kenya internalized that anger and let it take over until she could absolutely take no more. No one can make you angry unless you allow them to. Don't let other people's words corrupt your soul—it can be the source of a long-term problem. You may have been victimized because you were around people whose emotional repertory included being furious. The very thing that you are afraid of and work so hard to avoid is exactly what you attract. The same pattern will repeat itself with different circumstances and characters. What we neglected to mention about Kenya is that she grew up in a rough household and as a young girl solved her problems by fighting her way out of them. She eventually had to give up the physical fight to be able to get her life on track, but the anger was

*Kenya is not her real name.

still there. Her boss goaded her and wanted her to punch her in the face, but Kenya didn't do it. Thank God, because it wouldn't have been pretty. Her boss would have needed life support—literally. While Kenya was justifiably angry, she had to find a different resolution to her situation.

Are you always ready for a fight? Do you expect that someone wants to set you up or tear you down? Kenya did, and her boss was willing to oblige her. When we are angry and looking for a fight, we will get one. It may not be a physical altercation, but someone will come along and push those buttons. Be it a boss, a spouse, or your child, if you have swallowed that little angry pill someone will come along when it has taken full effect so watch out. So many times you hear in the media that black women are angry. It is thrown out there like a call and response. "Are you angry?" "Yes I am!"

We all can't be angry about the same thing, so for someone to say in a public forum that black women are angry is a broad statement. We have all been in a place where we were hurt or angry, but did we let it go? Did we learn the coping mechanisms to move past it so it won't happen again?

Don't get us wrong—we didn't say Kenya wasn't still angry; she just used other coping mechanisms to deal with the anger, which is a start. Does her former boss still get on her very last nerve? Yes. Does she have to deal with it directly now? No. She took the initiative, did the research, and provided an opportunity to create a position for herself after the resignation of another colleague.

What makes you angry? Can you connect that feeling to a prior emotion or situation? Candace, a normally peaceful person, gets extremely angry when she or someone close to her is disrespected. After talking about why she is so incensed by mere words, Candace realized the source of the anger. As a young child she came to America from Trinidad and was teased incessantly about her accent, mannerisms, and values for being an immigrant. She internalized the teasing and let the anger fester until she became a teenager and had a huge altercation with some girls in her neighborhood who attacked her because she was different. From that point on the slightest hint of disrespect brings out a very different Candace.

Spiritual Checkup

The funny thing about being on life support is many of us don't even know it. We walk around carrying all our undealt-with experiences, which are like diseases that destroy us on the inside, but leave us looking perfectly fine on the outside. There are many days when we have felt that our outside appearance doesn't even tell half of what's going on in our souls.

We have had the experience of handling a lot of emotional situations at once and can function as if it's business as usual. Despite all the things that go on, it's good to say, "Stop. Slow down and think about this for a minute." Or back people off because no matter what, if you look fine they will keep demanding more.

Women of color are amazing because we seem to be able to carry the weight of the world on our shoulders and still manage to say, "I can do that." Being able to realize you are taking on too much and not giving enough to yourself is a hard concept for us. Many of us will forgo taking care of ourselves to take care of others. We think going to church is enough to care for our souls. It is not. Caring for your soul is an every day, full-time thing. It's not just praying and worshiping, it is acting and living in that state. God has put you on this earth and kept you here because He has major plans for you. You have survived because some of the obstacles and challenges bestowed upon you enable you to rise to the occasion, and exercise the gift that He has given you. Why do we choose a life of less? Perhaps we are paralyzed by fear.

Maybe He wants you to make the most of your life now. "The Will of God will never take you where the Grace of God will not protect you." The power we give to our fear and to other people robs us of our true purpose in life. Give the power to God, let Him guide you. It is time to examine how we can transition from a state of living on life support to living in the peace, joy, and abundance we deserve!

SOUL REVEALING QUESTIONS

- What are the emotional, spiritual, and material needs in your life?

- Where do you go to meet those needs?

- Who provides support to you? Who can you call on in a moment of crisis?

- Who do you look to in order to share the truth about your life?

- Describe your emotional stability. Are you at your tipping point? Why?

- What does it take for you to trust?

- When have you chosen a life of less?

- What are you the most fearful of in your life?

- Are you bitter? What are the circumstances?

- How comfortable are you with yourself?

- How do you express yourself and your needs? How can you improve?

- What values are important to you? How do you incorporate them in your life?

Revelations Revealed:

I know of no better way to honor myself and create a loving and powerful relationship with myself than to eliminate my negative thought, release the bitterness, and eradicate the doubt. I choose to focus only on the gifts God has bestowed upon me and the mission I am here on earth to fulfill.

Your Revelations Revealed:

CHAPTER 2

Hold It! The Hold Back Factor

W hat is holding you back? What are the barriers that are preventing you from living the life you envision for yourself? Have you ever felt like when you have a new idea, goal, or positive plan, there is negative sonar seeking you out and trying to blow you out of the water? Stepping out of the box with an idea, a new direction in your life or business, leaves you vulnerable to attacks, sometimes from your closest family, friends, and colleagues. It will happen when you least expect it—opening day of your new business, the announcement of your engagement, your wedding day, the death or sickness of a loved one. "When it rains, it pours" is an old adage, but we have all felt it. We have news for you—it was not a coincidence.

Once you experience an attack in one part of your life, it makes it harder to maintain perspective and even more difficult to balance and handle the onslaught of crisis. It sometimes leaves us questioning our own sanity. "Am I crazy to think I can do this?" To avoid the pain and possible rejection, some of us live under the radar of life instead of choosing to just ignore the negativity and press on to fulfill our dreams. We all have the power to endure, but sometimes we just don't know it. Webster's Dictionary defines *endure* as: "to hold out against; suffer without yielding and to suffer patiently."

We are always taught to dig deep and push forward, but when our spirit suffers an attempted assassination it stops us in our tracks. Spiritual assault takes us off our focus and keeps us from doing what is best for ourselves. It can be the smallest thing, but it can be devastating to the psyche. Life is not unexpected, we're just unprepared. We have all heard "here today, gone tomorrow," but we don't take heed. It could be the smallest thing like an argument with your spouse, a minor car accident, or just a disagreement with a co-worker or your child that can take your focus away from doing what you need to do. So can you even imagine what a bigger event can do? A devastating flood, the death of a loved one, being fired from a job you thought you were doing well at. All these incidents are possible, but we never see them as probable so when they occur we are thrown off course.

The most common example of something small that can take us off our game is something we think we can all identify with in our lives at one time or another: dieting and exercise. We try to work out four times a week with an exercise partner, Antoinette, who is really committed. We eat pretty well— no meat, no bleached sugar, bread, or pasta, no soda or sugary juice, and lots of water. We rarely drink alcohol but if we do it will usually be a glass of wine. It sounds good, but here is where the little monkey wrench comes in. We go to the gym in the morning, but before we leave, our phones start ringing at 6:30 A.M.

Depending on what we may hear in conversation concerning business and our upcoming day, we can easily be distracted and somehow miss our time at the gym. Insignificant as it may seem, it leaves us feeling guilty for letting Antoinette and ourselves down. We can easily say we have to go, but sometimes it just doesn't seem that easy. While not cataclysmic, it makes us feel we are not focused and on our game.

The little things do matter. Going to the gym is one way to give to ourselves. It is our time and our goal. We want to be healthy, but if we let little things get in our way, we will constantly be sidetracked. We all get sidetracked and it is usually us who gets in our own way. We make excuses sometimes when it comes to the gym and we know it. It's easy to take time away from ourselves, but infinitely harder when someone else needs us. We know better than to think this way but it still happens and we have to ask ourselves why. Is it because we don't feel like we deserve to be healthy? We don't know how to make time for ourselves? All we know is that the little things can be symptoms of bigger events from our past.

How devastating it is when that thing holding us back isn't so small. Many times we have instances in our lives that take us off course for a long time. Candace was raised by a kind and wonderful man, her stepfather. But when it was time to go to college she excitedly asked her birth father, who her mother divorced when she was very young, if he would be able to help out with money for school, considering that her mom would have two kids in college at the same time.

Her birth father's reply was, "Honey, this world is not made for women. You are pretty, so why don't you just get married and not bother to go to college?"

With a smile he hopped in his car and never, ever provided any financial support for college. That was the end of their relationship. This one statement at such an impressionable age shaped her perception of marriage and, even more hurtful, herself. Candace felt that if she committed herself fully in a relationship, her father would be right. Maybe she really couldn't succeed without a husband. Just like any teenage girl, she was dealing with low self-esteem and unsure of what direction her life would take.

Although she had a traditional supportive family, they never knew about her father's comment, but also brought up the subject of marriage as if it was really important to them. No amount of awards, fellowships, or career achievements measured up to being married and having children. She pushed herself through her career, insisting on maximizing her experiences, traveling, working on the Olympics, but at one point in her life she hit a wall and didn't know why.

Subconsciously she was avoiding commitment and marriage, fearing that it would force her to give up her pursuit of a career and somehow prove that her birth father was right. What started developing was a pattern—over the years she dated men who had the same belief systems as her birth father.

At eighteen her first boyfriend told her that she would never make it without him. At twenty-one she found herself squaring off with a slightly older boyfriend who was twenty-nine who decided to tell her publicly on a street in Harlem—loudly, I may add—that he tried purposely to get her pregnant because it would calm her down. Or the man she was truly in love with for years who said that he couldn't continue a relationship with her because he wanted a simple wife and a simple life, not someone who wanted to pursue a career even if it benefited them as a family.

As time went on, the men were more sophisticated; it was the older boyfriend, sixteen years her senior, who admitted he had disdain for her career because it reminded him of the drive he once had but had to give up due to a stress-related illness. He claims to this day that he inadvertently tried to sabotage her career, almost causing her to lose her job. Or the surgeon who said he could not fall in love with her because he needed to have control. Candace came face-to-face time and time again with a duplicate of herself.

The pattern also continued into her business life. A former boss purposely blocked her from getting jobs elsewhere, but kept her on staff and was once overheard saying, "I won't tell her how good she is or she will get a big head." It even got personal when she attempted to buy a house from her high-profile friend and her husband who had moved up to a larger dwelling. He stopped the transaction once he found out Candace was the interested buyer, saying that she didn't have a husband so how could she ever afford this house.

Holding on to past hurts that are unresolved can be very traumatic. Your past experiences may influence you, but you are responsible for who you are here and now. The process of examining the past and remedying the present is the next step in getting to the healing revelation. We all have things that hold us back in a space and time—we become immobilized. For Candace, was it the moment she became completely past it? No, but she is aware of it now and can change the way she interacts with her current love interests. A mentor once told her, "I've come to believe men have a limited view of what can be, especially if it wasn't their idea. But I think you know that I, you, and most of the women we know walk so far past others' expectations." By hearing these words she has created a new way of thinking about what she is capable of and what she deserves.

Grasshopper in a Jar

From the small things to the major issues, we can all be held back from being the best and most efficient women we can be. Why do some women choose to suffer through much of their lives while others seem to flourish? Dr. Jarralynne Agee, a Performance Consultant and Psychologist at UC Berkeley, call this the "grasshopper in a jar" feeling that many women suffer through. "In some areas of her life she feels trapped and unable to see a viable option for a better standard of living.

"Because she can't imagine anything better for herself, just like the grasshopper, she goes about convincing herself that her surroundings, the few blades of grass, the occasional morsel of food, and the one rock in the corner is actually not a bad habitat. She begins to acclimate to the lower standard. She begins to believe that this is the best she can have. Many women do that in their lives today, finding ourselves in a situation that is far beneath our potential."

Mrs. Doubtfire

You may be living a disconnected life, feeling that you have no connection to success or happiness. It is almost easier living this way; it alleviates the disappointment and dulls the pain. Disconnection is a symptom of doubt. Doubt about the future, doubt about who you are. Am I a good enough _____? Did I make the right decision about _____? When doubt creeps in, it is a lonely place. There is not one person on this earth who has not lived with or struggled with doubt. Doubt is that little misstep in our stride that makes us question our abilities.

When we began putting our first book together many people doubted us. Our families didn't believe us, our friends thought we were crazy, and business colleagues questioned our ability to actually pull it off. We persevered and even if we had doubt in our own minds, we had each other to pull us through. People think haters are bad, but it is doubters that really attack your soul. Haters just hate and are very upfront with their intentions, but doubters can be very close friends who spread the disease of doubt that undermines you.

Doubters utilize others as a personal litmus test for their own abilities or inabilities. "How can she pull that off when I can't even imagine getting out of my nine-to-five job?!" It's the limits they put on themselves that they try to bestow on others. Chances are you may have been the Mrs. Doubtfire, urging others to take the safe road, because you are too scared to jump out there yourself or simply just afraid of being left behind. Like a fire, that doubt spreads until it is extinguished.

Excuse Me, Miss

The ugly cousin of doubt is excuse. Sometimes what we can't see is scarier than the gruesome truth we live every day. It is easier to make an excuse for why we can't change than it is to actually change. Change requires us to acknowledge our faults and missteps and that in itself is extremely painful. For some, making excuses comes as easy as opening their mouths. Some women have an excuse for everything and a solution for nothing.

Excuses mask what is really going on. We have worked with many people who have made excuses for one thing or another. We've even made excuses ourselves. One particular instance that comes to mind concerns a friend of ours who wholeheartedly committed to doing a project for us. She was enthusiastic and seemed highly motivated, but when the time came to perform the task she was full of excuses about why she couldn't pull it off. It was everyone else's fault the project wasn't completed. She went from personal excuses to the professional and even made an excuse about us. When we called her on everything she broke down, claiming that she was sorry for not being able to deliver what she promised because she was simply scared of the scope of the project.

Instead of speaking about her fear she made excuses. We would have understood if she told us she was afraid, but after the fact, when we spent a large amount of money on something we couldn't use, we didn't want to hear the excuses. It caused a rift in our relationship with her, all because she was scared and too afraid to admit it. Perhaps she felt more comfortable doing a project that didn't exercise her creativity and take her professional skills to the next level.

Your choices regarding the people in your life may seem like conscious decisions, but that may not necessarily be so. We easily attract people who remind us of those memories. If you were told all your life that you were not beautiful or smart, you attract people who reinforce or trigger those hot buttons. When we confronted our friend about her excuses she told us we reminded her of her mother, who told her to stop making excuses and live up to her potential.

Are You Comfortable?

The common denominator in every situation you face is yourself. Dr. Elisabeth Jackson-English, a clinical social worker specializing in family-and-relationship therapy, says, "Some women don't believe we deserve better, we are not as driven as we need to be. We lack focus and get comfortable with our current existence. The belief that we don't deserve better is reinforced by many factors, i.e. past experiences, environment, historical oppression, sexism, and racism. It is further impacted by our own self-doubt. It is that old saying, 'We are our worst enemy.' "

Being comfortable with our current state is a combination of all the things we've talked about that are symptoms of what may be holding us back as women of color. Doubt, excuses, and fear make us stay in the glass jar like the grasshopper. We adapt and therefore make ourselves comfortable. "I am happy with my weight—so what if I weigh 250 pounds. My man likes it!" Or, "It doesn't matter that I didn't get that promotion," or, "I can't go back to school because I have a baby."

What drives you? Are you motivated by money, power, sex, comfort, or all of the above? What drives us can determine how far we are able to go, and if you are driven by comfort, some may argue you have no drive at all. Dr. English says, "We are not driven: from a psychological standpoint this again is created by everything from low self-esteem, depression, poor motivation, and simply not knowing how to begin. Did you know that three percent of all the people in the world control eighty percent of the wealth? That is because most people are taught to think along the lines of getting an education, and then a job. This in itself can drastically reduce the drive to think out of the box and move to the next level. Jobs offer security, and the more secure you are, the less motivated you are to achieve greater things, which can hold you back in so many aspects of your life."

We are driven by the same thing when it comes to our business: to empower women of color. Separately, we are motivated by different things. Determining what drives you to do the things you do is an important factor in figuring out what may be holding you back. For example, we know a woman who decided to get pregnant to compete with her boyfriend's wife. Yes, his wife. So now she's pregnant, he's in denial, and his wife is oblivious to the situation. The woman was driven to "get her man," and now she is wondering what she is going to do because this is their second child and he's still married.

Instead of being focused on caring for herself and her two-year-old daughter, she was focused on trying to keep her married boyfriend. Says Dr. English, "We lack focus: again, there are many factors that contribute to this. Once one has determined there is no physiological or psychological reason, which includes anything from hormonal imbalances to substance abuse, then the only thing to say is that societal demands have made it increasingly more difficult for people to focus when they're trying to keep food on the table. The distractions of living in today's world are overwhelming, from TV to cell phones and video games—they all take away from human interaction and weaken our focus on self, family, and financial freedom."

To put it simply, we get comfortable. "Most of what people do on a daily basis, they do without thinking because they fall into patterns. Most people are disenchanted with their current circumstances, but most of the time it takes some great impetus, often negative, to get them to decide it's time for a change," suggests Dr. English.

At the core of our behavior are the same patterns and practices that we seem to repeat throughout our lives, coping styles that we adopt and adapt to as children or adults, which are often self-defeating. According to Dr. Jeffery Young, "Coping styles are the ways the child adapts to schemas, or emotional memories deeply entrenched in our psyches." If you suffered a devastating loss of a significant person in your life, it is embedded into your brain. When you revisit those memories, they become even more internalized.

Once Upon a Time . . .

So what is it that really holds us back? We are born into a story, and as we get older we create stories about ourselves and then we act them out. The belief in the story and the ownership of the story is what keeps us denying our true potential. Many of us are told things by people we trust that are detrimental to our souls. Consciously or subconsciously, we agree with the story and perpetuate the myth. Were you ever told you were an "oops" baby, or a love child? Or perhaps that they worked really hard to have you, and the list goes on and on. Those stories and our belief in them leave us spiritually and emotionally scarred and unable to move forward to live a full life of peace and happiness.

Tyra grew up believing a story about who she was. From birth she was told that she was her mother's daughter. She had two older sisters and a happy life. She adored her mother and looked up to her sisters, and then one day everything changed. A woman came to the door and said, "Hi, baby! You look so beautiful. I'm your mother and I love you." Confused,

Tyra thought this lady must be on drugs. It turned out the lady had been on crack, but was really her mother and had recently completed a short stay in rehab. The woman she knew as her mother was really her grandmother and her sisters were really her aunts. Tyra was devastated. She withdrew from her family and began a downward spiral of drug abuse and self-destruction.

Tyra is still trying to deal with the truth that she knew versus the lie she was told. She is now in a juvenile detention center and trying to overcome her addictions.

Some people don't know they are lying because they invest in the story and begin to believe it. Tyra's grandmother believed it was better for Tyra to think she was her mother than tell her the truth. It made her feel like she was protecting both her babies: her oldest daughter and her only granddaughter. She never understood that there would be devastating consequences for everyone involved.

The story you may have been told may not have been so elaborate, but may have caused just as much personal devastation. Your complicity in the story is what makes it so harmful. Whether the story is about your looks, how smart you are or aren't, the list is endless and the stories create your beliefs about yourself. Our beliefs in these stories we are told hold us back from improving the future. To deny the story is to say we were wrong, or we wasted time, or we were gullible and naive. Any way you slice it, it doesn't make us feel good about who we are or the choices we've made. We must learn to submit to the greater truth of who we are because innately we know the truth. Whether it is a whisper, or a scream, we hear the truth—it is just a simple matter of listening.

Toxic Waste

What holds many of us back is the fact that we actively engage in toxic relationships. We knowingly invite people into our lives who try to tear us down. Do you find yourself giving everyone in your circle advice, but when something happens in your life they have nothing to offer? They look at you with blank faces, like they just don't know or, even worse, could care less. You want to help yourself, but at what cost?

In our travels with *Souls of My Sisters*, we saw countless women who told us that we inspired them and that some of the things we were doing—sharing a message, writing a best-selling book, and touring the country—were things that they wanted to do, too. Invariably, one of us would say, "Then do it now." And then the excuses would come, explaining why they couldn't do it. While we listened we couldn't help but notice that of all the excuses that we heard, no one stopped to think that we might have used the same excuses, too. Sometimes we trick ourselves into believing that successful people have some sort of magic wand that fixes things in their lives and that they don't face the same issues that other people experience. Well, we are here to tell you that there is no quick fix—otherwise, this book would have been called *The Magic Wand.* Knowing there are ways to fix things in our lives is a secret that we couldn't keep to ourselves.

There is one secret that we can share, and this is a big one. If you want to see what's broken in your life, look no further than your own backyard. We have been friends for over three decades and our friendship has typical ups and downs, but what it has consistently had is a built-in support network for one another. What's significant about having solid friendships is that a support system will help you weather the storms that are sure to come. A good support system can do more than just help you get by; the right friends can make or break you.

Remember how our parents used to screen our friends? They'd decide who was good enough for us. Well, there is something to that concept. People who are successful at life surround themselves with other people who are successful. W.E.B. DuBois, the famed African-American scholar, had a concept called the "talented tenth." He recognized that an elite number of African-Americans were making great strides on behalf of our race, and what's even more interesting, they were all connected in some way, through college, social organizations, or spiritual affiliations. It's no trick or surprise that great people are drawn to each other. Take a look at your circle. Are these people movers and shakers or are they the brakes on the wheels? Your associates don't just have a powerful impact on your career and professional status—they have an even bigger impact on how you see yourself.

"If you are the smartest person in your group, get a better group." Les Brown

Toxic Friends

Many of us have heard the phrase, "I am my own worst enemy," and that is true for so many of us. We are highly critical of ourselves to the point that we sabotage growth and success in our lives. However, if you took an inventory of your life and found that the person who would be an even greater critic of your goals is a person other than yourself, then that is a red flag. What kind of friend is that?

It's hard to discern the people on your side versus the people who are thorns in your side. That's because emotions, history, and habit keep us tied to these people who are the naysayers. Dr. Jarralynne Agee, a psychologist at University of California, Berkeley, calls the people who fill that bill the "nonbelievers." The nonbelievers are toxic friends who tell you you can't when you know that you can. They tell you how many times you've fallen and lose track of how many times you get up. According to Dr. Agee, these people serve very little positive purpose in your life; however, you serve a critical role in theirs. Many toxic friends use you as a comparative measure to make them feel better about their own lives. As long as they can find flaws in you, they can ignore their own shortcomings.

Be careful about pointing the finger at someone you think is a toxic friend in your life. Remember that misery loves company and like attracts like. You and your toxic friend may be peas in a pod. It may be that instead of being peer mentors you might just be in peer misery together. If your conversations start off with what's bad and end with what is worse, that might just be a clue that you are in a relationship that gives more airtime to the bad than the good.

Losing friends can be like losing your foundation and sometimes even your roots. Toxic people can be lovers, friends, co-workers, and family members. Our suggestion is not that you let those people go but instead first try transforming your way of thinking and behaving to allow them to be the resource and support that you do need. We have met with people who have come from the harsh streets of the ghetto to working in multimillion-dollar businesses. Their success is dependent on being fully immersed in their new situation.

However, calls from home, late-night visits from their "Cousin Ray," and frequent messages from the 'hood come streaming back into these busy executives' lives. The information that might come through may be depressing, distracting, and overwhelming. But we shouldn't just cut people off. If they were our original foundation somewhere in our lives, they are part of the fabric of who we are. We shouldn't cut them off but we should definitely minimize the impact of their negativity. So, how do we move on without selling out? First of all, by recognizing that whatever good you create for yourself makes you more of a resource for the people in your life who need you.

The people in your life who don't lift you up but would rather pull you down may deserve your consideration but you do not owe them your happiness. The key to weeding out the nonbelievers starts with asking you the questions on the Toxic Friend Test that we developed with Dr. Agee.

THE TOXIC FRIEND TEST

1. When I get done talking to this friend, how do I feel?
   a. Encouraged
   b. Discouraged
   c. Distracted

2. If I am having a great day and I take their call, how do I expect to feel?
   a. Even better.
   b. Let down.
   c. Nothing at all.

3. When I am faced with a tough situation, I call them
   a. First
   b. Last
   c. I'll leave a message but they won't call back.

4. You've finally gotten up the nerve to make a big change. You call your friend and the response will be
   a. How can I help?
   b. Don't try it.
   c. They tell you about their big change.

5. You are beating yourself up about a mistake you made.
    They

    a. Help you problem-solve for the next time.
    b. Remind you of your pattern of mistakes.
    c. Say, "You'll be all right," and change the subject.

Scoring

Give each answer the following scores, a: 5; b: 0; c: 2.
Add up the points and read the results below.

Results

25–18 Your friend is a Believer

Help keep them that way by being supportive of them, too,
by making plans to go over each other's goals. Use them as a
problem-solving partner when things go wrong and as a
cheering section when you hit the mark. Keep their energy
going by returning the favor and providing structure rather
than stress when they need you.

17–10 Your friend is a Peer Supporter

This friend is not yet a Believer, but don't discount them
just yet, either. With a little bit of work you can turn this person from one of your confidantes into one of your best sup-
porters. Before you make a decision about what they can do
for you, check to make sure that their own distractions aren't
keeping them from being the friend that you need. If you no-

tice that their needs trump yours, then back off for the moment and stand by your friend. Focusing on what they need right now helps you to build a better friendship and provides the added bonus of letting you experience some issues so that when it's your turn to work through something, you have some insight to draw from. Give more than take for a little while longer and see if this doesn't boost your friend up to the Believer section where each of you gains from your interactions with one another. If you try it for six months and the friend isn't ready to reciprocate and/or it feels like a drain on you, then your friend might just have slipped into the nonbeliever category. If things get better, consider yourself lucky and keep working at it because this friend is a keeper.

9–below The Toxic Friend

Pretend you are on a high-school football team. You are getting on the bus and you take your band, your cheerleaders, and the pep squad from your rival school. Right? Wrong! Your confidante, the nonbeliever, is just like the pep squad from the other team. When you have a plan they disrupt it. When you need someone to cheer, they boo. Even when you have your own positive thoughts or someone else in your life says something positive, it's as if they drown out your cheering section with their own negativity. But that is not the problem. Your desire and need to keep this toxic friend in your life is the problem. There is a phrase, "partner in crime," for a reason. People that hang together in a negative way go down together the same way. If your friend is the one tying your laces in a knot before the big game it may be time to let them go.

Unlike the Peer Supporter, it may not be worth it to put a lot of energy into trying to reform the relationship. Okay, you care about this person a lot, and we know that you really want to try to make things better.

Try to do that, and then come back and read the rest of this paragraph. Or maybe you have already tried to make it work and saw that it didn't get better. You still don't feel encouraged around this friend. You aren't at your best when you are together and sometimes you, and this toxic friend lead to bad decisions and bad outcomes. When you come back to this paragraph after trying to make things work with this toxic friend, you will find that the best thing you can do for this friend is remove yourself from the picture. Not because you don't care anymore, but because you care so much that you'd prefer a powerful positive connection with someone who has meant so much to you over time. Take the hit, let this relationship go for now, and pray over it. In time, expect something different to grow in the place of what was once there.

Often we seek mirrors of ourselves who exaggerate our weaknesses and allow us to remain complacent. If you are critical or insecure and you know these are two of your weaknesses, you should stay away from people who also exhibit these same tendencies. There are more naysayers in this world than you or we wish to count. They are the friends who call you and continuously dump their problems on you. When you try to help in any way, they fight you. "You think you are better than me." Or, "How do you know that will work?" or, "You just don't understand!" Some of you are reading this and shaking your heads because this has happened to you too many times.

You can find toxic people in every area of your life. Their intentions may be good, but the way they treat you is totally unacceptable. It may not seem like it takes much away from your spirit, but day after day, month after month, and year after year it is like a slow leak in a tire, eventually leaving you emotionally deflated. We're sure you have met a toxic co-worker or boss, relative or friend, child or spouse. How you deal with these toxic people determines whether these people are holding you back or watching your dust. Unfortunately, for the most part we get sucked into the drama.

Let Me Entertain You

Do you like to laugh? Do you like to be mesmerized by a stunt or watch a good television show? Most of us love to be entertained. We watch television, go to the movies, or even get an up-close and personal show from our friends and family. Chances are if you like to be entertained, you invite drama into your life. You either watch the drama unfold or you insert yourself into it by providing an opinion or actually interjecting. Being part of the drama stops you from moving forward because you get stuck in the role you are playing. Like a soap opera with many characters, everyone plays a part and sometimes the more outlandish the role, the more we interject ourselves, making it impossible to detach from the situation. Drama is a key hold-back factor because it's so easy to get sucked into a drama that doesn't necessarily involve you. It's like the Pied Piper tooting away on his flute—you get lulled by the sound of the voices and the cacophony of the chaos. Why do you think all of the Maurys, Jerrys, Court TV, and reality television invasion has been so successful? America is watching and can't seem to get enough of the fights, bickering, paternity tests, incestuous relationships, hair-pulling, bar-brawling DRAMA.

Are You a Fire Woman, Police Woman, or a Nurse?

It is difficult to save people. When we engage in toxic relationships we oftentimes play the role of rescuer. We are the ones who choose to put on the uniform, roll up our sleeves, and say, "Here I come to save the day!"

Are you the Fire Woman who is always putting out the fires? Are you the one who everyone goes to as the mediator? The Fire Woman feels the need to stop the chaos, but in effect becomes the center of it and gets attacked in turn. We're not trying to say that you shouldn't offer advice in the middle of a heated argument, but you shouldn't find yourself in this role often and when you do you must know when to exit the building for your own safety.

Or are you the Police Woman? Do you find yourself always laying down the law and telling people what to do? The Police Woman assumes the responsibility of being the boss of everyone. The Police Woman interjects even when her services are not needed. She butts in and takes over, telling everyone what to do and how to do it. It's not bad to have an opinion or an idea; what is bad is that you are imposing yourself on others when you could be working on you.

Lastly, could you be the Nurse, always caring for someone else's problems? Do you always lend that ear and let someone cry on your shoulder? Do you live to help them mend their problems and bandage their broken hearts? The Nurse gives so much of herself to helping others that she rarely finds time to help herself. She goes around trying to give every last bit of energy she has to everyone else and leaves none for herself. It is wonderful to help others, but you can only truly assist them if you are on good terms with your own soul.

You can't save the world, though some of us try. None of these roles are bad—it is the amount of time that you spend in them that allows toxic relationships to form. What's worse is you are actually the one who needs saving from these relationships. Toxic souls prey on you; they float through life, and when they sense that you may be glowing like a heated missile they seek you out to destroy your spirit. So many times we've heard people say, "I heard you do publicity—can you help me get on Oprah?" "I heard you write books. I have an idea—will you write my book for me?" Don't get us wrong—we love to give advice, but we can't do what someone needs to do for themselves.

Connection to negative people forms co-dependent relationships that leave you feeling seemingly more grounded and in control of your own life and allows you to believe it is good enough just to be okay. You may be addicted to being the rescuer because the role overshadows your own flaws and by default you won't be able to deal with your own issues. The co-dependents weigh you down and set you on a path to making you an unwitting participant in your own demise. Those qualities will rub off on you quite easily.

The brother of a friend of ours, who wishes to remain anonymous, was diagnosed with a serious mental illness—yet he was a combination of charming and cunning and was an expert at manipulating his parents and siblings. His parents were, of course, in denial, as so many parents are, because no one wants to believe that their child may have a mental illness. His siblings knew better than anyone what he was capable of and now had a medical diagnosis to prove it. They approached him about his latest shenanigans, which we don't recommend, but they insisted on squaring off. Heated words were exchanged and it was this one statement that stopped them in their tracks: "Crazy is contagious, and I want you to come closer to me because if you so much as brush against me I will have you arrested." Are you kidding me? He was right—he was spreading his craziness, and they permitted him to engage them in a hostage situation as they tried to make sense out of his toxic nonsense. What was worse, he was willing to get the police involved. His siblings immediately took stock, and got him out of their lives immediately.

Toxicity comes in all forms. It could be your seemingly sweet boyfriend who can sense when you are pulling away and gets sick each time you decide you want to end the relationship. We have heard and experienced it—it runs the gamut, until you wise up and say enough is enough. It can be painful to cut the ties with someone you love, but the less time you spend with this person, the more you will be able to regain your sanity.

Declaring Your Independence

The "at least" exercise is a place to start to help you see the limiting thoughts that impact the way you see yourself. Are there areas in your life where you excel but others where you feel less secure? Could it be possible that the way you are looking at the situation is actually impacting the outcome? Studies have shown that if we have low expectations of our children, they will rise to meet the lowest possible standard of what we expect. Instead, children who have parents who have very high expectations are more likely to succeed and in some cases even exceed the expectations. It takes more than an encouraging word and a pat on the back, but the first step is changing your outlook as well as the way you talk about your life.

You have a destiny that needs to be fulfilled, and you will not be able to do it if you are weighed down with unnecessary and exhausting people. Make room for God's divine grace to fill you up and energize you as you work toward your ultimate destination.

SOUL REVEALING QUESTIONS

- What doubts do you struggle with?

- Explain significant past hurts, misunderstandings, and grudges that you feel are holding you back.

- What past hurt do you believe is your greatest barrier?

- What is the most vulnerable part of your life?

- What could someone do to make you able to talk about your concerns, anger, weaknesses, pain, and struggles?

- Who do you believe has disappointed you or told you a negative story about yourself in your lifetime?

- Is there a relationship that you believe should be mended?

Revelations Revealed:

God has provided the sun to nourish you so you can grow. You know exactly the purpose God has for you. You deserve the opportunity to take charge of your life and be whoever you hope and pray to be. Women are judged by our performance, whereas men are judged by their potential. Be very clear about your potential if you have not started on your path; know and face the fact that you have your eyes, heart, and soul on greatness. It is sometimes so powerful and blinding that it is easier for you to run back into your comfort zone. You may ask yourself what is so special about you? You were given your special gift to contribute to mankind. Part of your mission is to gain knowledge through self-development and to concentrate on your goals. Be open to the lessons placed in your life each and every day. We close ourselves off, believing we already have the knowledge, and go full steam ahead with our plans. Wherever your journey takes you, a guarantee for a life filled with purpose and joy is to commit to living each day with God's power and love. We all deserve a healing revelation . . . As Robert Collier said, "Your chances of success in any undertaking can always be measured by your belief in yourself."

Your Revelations Revealed:

CHAPTER 3

Soul Survival

When you watch, let's say, a Lifetime movie and some-one is on life support, you see a dramatized personal fight for survival. These stories take you on an emotional roller-coaster. We can be objective about the stories on the television screen, but what happens when that person is you? There are no lights or cameras but there is certainly plenty of action. There is a person literally fighting to hold it together, facing her worst fears, and finding out the truth despite the story she was told. Whether you are fighting to keep a mar-riage together, were there when the levees broke, are working on understanding your child, or just simply crying out to God to save you, your survival instinct will kick in.

You feel battered, and you may fall into a depression, or you may fight. Whether it is betrayal, bad choices, or an un-foreseen circumstance, life has just landed with a big thump. The amazing thing about us as women of color is it doesn't matter how down-and-out we may seem—our innate will to survive keeps us going. Our souls literally cry out to be healed—it's what keeps us going. Tapping into that instinct to survive is the beginning of the revelation.

Tracie Frank Mayer's Story

What would you do if you were faced with the unthinkable as you look into your thirteen-day-old baby boy's eyes and find out he was born incompatible with nature and could possibly die.

"What did he say, Helmut?" I sensed the Professor's eyes on me as I spoke. "Spricht ihre Frau Deutsch?" he asked my husband. Helmut shook his head. "Nein," he said. With his hand still to his forehead, his elbow now supported by the examination table where our son lay, Helmut raised his free hand and groped for mine. He turned and looked up at me, tears brimmed his eyes. . . .

Experiences, occurrences, situations befall all of us. This is a fact of life, of our existence as we know it. Still, I never imagined I would find myself a continent away living in Germany far from the security of family and friends facing a doctor who would look me straight in the eye and in faltering English, tell me my perfectly healthy-looking thirteen-day-old baby was born incompatible with nature and would die any minute.

The heart has four chambers through which blood is pumped. The upper two chambers are referred to as the right atrium. The lower two, the right and left ventricles. My son was born with a single atrium and a single ventricle, as well as pulmonary artesia whereby there is no connection between the heart and the pulmonary arteries. And as a result of him lacking a main pulmonary artery, there existed basically the absence of a normal cardiac structure. This haunting confusion is known in the medical community as Heterotaxy Syndrome. Essentially, Marc drew each precious breath from a beating heart comprised of two chambers rather than four.

The gist of survival is coping. Enduring life altering events can indeed be so challenging that even the very thought of confronting such ends of the earth's adversity can seem to be an insurmountable task.

I didn't discover any written rules when I found myself in a duel with the fates. I could only hope for an uneasy truce as time and again I asked myself just how does one emerge from the depths of distress and despair and look heavenward when fear and uncertainty fall like rain all around? How are we to rustle up the strength and the courage to pick up the pieces and reassemble the picture of a rainbow when our world staggers under the strain of death's knell?

The possibility of our son dying submerged my husband and me into a black bottomless pit of finality where irretrievable loss and remorse cocooned and the "wish I would haves" and "what ifs"; a godforsaken place of no atonement, no chance to make amends.

I fell to my knees by his crib and begged God to help me and to take care of our child, to lift this burden of grief that was slowly killing me, to fill this empty room with the joy and happiness deserving of it. My baby, my baby, my baby. "Sweet Jesus," I prayed, "please take care of our baby, take care of our baby . . . and help Helmut and me through this."

The bottom line of my son's prognosis was clear to me. It's just that rigor mortis had stiffened the perspectives of the cardiologists where he lay at the University of Cologne Hospital and I didn't live in that world. For two months they chanted their refrain that "Marc will die, will die." But Marc didn't die and didn't die and I knew I had to give God a hand in this miracle. Through a lifelong friend of my father's, my parents found a surgeon in a neighboring town who believed he could help my son—at least for a while. At two months and seven days Marc underwent the first of his heart surgeries: a left sided Blalock Taussig shunt.

The following July found Marc and me back in our home town at the University of Cologne Hospital for our first check up since the surgery. Certain we were over the hump, I dared to toss worry to the dust heap and whoop it up! The following morning found me baffled and barely breathing when the cardiologist told me that Marc's oxygen level was still dangerously low. I'd done all I could and I felt so powerless. A welter of emotions, primarily a searing anger at the injustice of it all overwhelmed me. We'd come so far and still not far enough, and I was so afraid of the unknowns lying in wait and just how many of these surgical procedures my baby could endure. Slipping deeper into a vortex of fear, I tried to get a grip on my disbelief. I didn't want sugar plums, just an affirmation—and not one scrawled in invisible ink of a future where all would be well. Marc's cry charged the air. It was a declaration that I'd best discard the notion of a perfectly predictable life and had better start enjoying every minute of the present, because it— the here and now—is the only thing truly available. And it is fleeting.

A puncture of the right artery set the stage for the heart catheterization one month later confirming the fact that Marc would indeed undergo another Blalock Taussig operation, this time on the right side, here at this Cologne Hospital. He was thirteen months old.

My insides often curdled with fear. I kept a peace of mind stocked medicine cabinet and tried to go by guess and by God. But it wasn't easy. Perhaps the worst was the feeling of not having a doctor, one who could feed you the soothing syrup, give you an inkling of hope. Though I felt like I was always swinging on tenterhooks, I often dared to feel victorious because The Hammer hadn't fallen and I felt like I'd been moving mountains fighting off this virus and the virus afflicting my child and he was alive!!! And then a nay-saying doctor would chant his refrain. So I kept talking to God. Though I was often scared to death, especially during those wee hours of the morning when the demons would be on their worst behavior clawing at my back, I knew I could not allow fear to coerce me into submission. On many days I had to take it minute by minute. But deep in my heart, I knew that for the sake of my son, I could not wallow in what could not help me. His life depended on it.

In grade school, I swooped Marc up in my arms and carried him on class field trips and as discreetely as I could, carried his school bag up to his classroom on the third floor. Because he couldn't do sports, I had him instructed in Tai Chi. I enrolled him in a swimming class and amazingly he took to water like a fish. He learned to play the piano and I was very strict about his school work. There was no room for self-pity. How could there be if he really didn't see himself any differently than the other kids?

It was extremely important to me that he be mentally strong and self-confident. And fearless.

I kicked the covers away the morning of January 5, 1994 in a state of premonition panic. Marc had been growing progressively weaker over the last months, more short of breath. Marc's cardiologist would be waiting for us at eleven o'clock.

"His shunts sound good . . . I don't think we have to do anything right now, but the time is coming when we will have to decide—"

"Well, what does right now mean? How much time do we have?" I asked him.

"It could be soon, very soon, or it could be one month or six months from now."

"Well, what kind of operation will the surgeon want to do?" I asked.

He gaze dropped to the table and he said, "I don't know. We won't know until we open him up."

That was the wrong answer. It went way, way beyond the pale of my understanding.

A couple days later, Helmut drove to Hanover for a floor-covering fair. He would be there for two days. During that time I had an appointment by my gynecologist for my half yearly pap smear (I'd had surgery for precancerous cells in my uterus at the same time Marc had his first surgery but only under the condition that it would be carried out at the same hospital), an appointment to get our dog's teeth cleaned, and for Marc to get his DPT shot, then attend Lydia's birthday party. That still left me too much time to crawl up inside myself and implode. I told Helmut I'd go to the store in between all my running around and keep an eye on things.

I took a seat that Wednesday afternoon several feet away from the front desk. I pulled an issue of *Good Housekeeping* magazine from my purse. Flipping through the pages I came upon a booklet. The title said "The 400 Best Doctors in America." I quickly turned the pages to cardiac surgery. I decided to write to two of these surgeons: Dr. Aldo Castaneda because it said in brackets after his name and Children's Hospital, Boston, Massachusetts, of those with congenital problems 90 percent of patients are children. The other doctor was Dr. Albert Starr, of St. Vincent's Hospital in Portland. I chose him because Oregon is close to my home state. So I sat down and I hand wrote the same letter twice:

January 14, 1994

Dear Dr. _____,

My name is Tracie Frank-Mayer. I am an American living in Cologne, Germany. At this time Marc is nine years old. As you can see by his medical reports he has had two palliative surgeries. With his hemoglobin values rising, the doctors believe the time again is approaching for us once again to prepare for surgery. With this limited information here Dr. _____, is it possible that you could suggest a particular operative procedure that would be beneficial to my son?

I am sincerely grateful for your time and attention, and a healthy happy New Year from my family to yours,

Tracie

On January 20, 1994, I received a letter from Dr. Starr. It read in part:

. . . Potentially Marc is a candidate for what we call a Fontan reconstruction . . . I would suggest that you have a recent echocardiogram done . . . be in touch about whether a Fontan is possible.

My hopes soared.

A couple of nights later the telephone rang.

"Hello?"

"Yes, hello," a voice said. "May I speak with Tracie Mayer?"

"Yes, this is she speaking," I said.

"This is Dr. Castaneda calling from Boston"—stunned I gripped the phone as he continued to speak, "I've seen variations in the heart malformation your son has and I think we might be able to help him."

A few minutes had passed before the realization struck me that one of America's best doctors had just personally called me offering the hope of Nirvana. The first time since Marc had emerged from my womb.

On May 2, 1994, God held and guided Doctor Castaneda's hands in the miracle I fought so hard for and so much believed in.

Tracie turned a negative around with her faith and to inspire others she's detailing her life's journey in her memoir entitled, Ever heard of Heterotaxy Syndrome? Well, neither had I . . .

Tracie wants every mother to know that they are not alone when they are facing a difficulty with a child whether it is a challenge or an illness.

When we think about our physical instinct to survive we think about a physical threat to our existence. We are dependent on our ability to be alert to physical threats. We are even alert to a perceived physical threat. We have a thing about personal space. We don't like it when people enter our personal space uninvited. We perceive it instinctively as a threat. It doesn't necessarily have to be a real threat, even a perceived threat will cause us to brace ourselves and ready our minds and bodies for defense. We take no chances when it comes to our bodies or the physical protection of our loved ones. So why is it we actually invite the threats to our souls into our lives freely and let them attack us daily until we are depleted?

Most of the time we walk around with the attitude, "That's so sad, but it won't happen to me." We look at situations as if they have nothing to do with us because somehow we seem immune to the pain and suffering that people around us are experiencing. As women of color, we oftentimes want to distance ourselves from others' pain as if it is somehow contagious. If we reach out and help it might happen to us, or better yet, if we reach out and help, the pain will feel very real and we will become vulnerable.

Recently, Candace was going through a rough situation that was a real attack on her soul. She was hurt, angry, and confused about how she ended up in the middle of a political situation that was very public. We're talking about a national news public, but because of legal reasons we can't discuss— but it had absolutely nothing to do with her. I helped Candace through the situation and together we were able to tease out what was really going on and get her to a place of power so she could deal with the situation. What was so surprising was how grateful Candace was to me for pitching in. She was almost overwhelmed by my love and support. We have been friends for over twenty years and for me to see her in pain is like me being in pain, too. Needless to say, I was a little shocked by her reaction to what I view as our everyday relationship.

What we began to understand was that regardless of what people say about what you may be going through, many don't try to help solve the problem.

We are incredibly busy people and to help someone else whose soul is being attacked takes time and true emotional connection. Some of us have become so numb to feeling that we are unable to connect to someone else's problems because we can barely connect to our own. Attacks on our souls are more subliminal than any physical attack. Combined with the stories we've been told about ourselves by our family, friends, and society, constant attacks on our souls are what deplete our faith and lead us into needing life support. We feel detached from others and our true soul connections with our friends and family become weakened.

There are many situations where we actually open our lives to people who attack our souls. Case in point—our friend Teri. She couldn't wait to tell us about her fine new man. He didn't have much, but she knew she could mold him into the perfect husband. After years of time and effort Teri got exactly what she wanted. Marriage, three beautiful children, and was able to steer her husband into the healthcare field and into a lucrative position. She seemed to have a fairy tale life. They had recently bought a new house, but inside, their relationship was rocky at best. Although he did everything to please Teri she always set the bar higher for herself and her family. He also grappled with self-loathing issues due to a former life in the street and abandonment by his mother. Through meeting Teri he was able to turn his life around. Appearing to be the gorgeous storybook couple, they were invited to several celebrity-driven events by Teri's successful friends.

When she took her husband to these events he would have outbursts and make public scenes because he didn't feel comfortable in that environment. He became elusive, leaving Teri feeling suspicious and insecure. After numerous incidents and disappearances, especially an unexplained four-day trip to the Bahamas, Candace suggested that Teri hire a private investigator to see what was actually going on with her husband. One night after the investigation was completed the investigator asked Teri to meet him in front of a hospital in New York City. When she pulled up in her friend's car she saw her husband in his car waiting for someone outside the hospital.

Out walks what the investigator later told her was his girlfriend who worked at this hospital. Teri watched as the woman got in the car and kissed her husband on the lips. Enraged, Teri got out and walked over to the car. Her husband said, "Get away from the car!" Teri screamed, "But I'm your wife!" He put the car in drive, and in an effort to stop him, Teri jumped on the hood of the car. He then, with the girlfriend screaming, "What are you doing?!" proceeded to get on the highway with his wife still on the hood of the car. Her friends, in shock, followed in their car, screaming and honking the horn for him to stop. He finally stopped in between exits, where she jumped off the car and slapped him. Come to find out he lied to his girlfriend and told her he was a single doctor.

Teri was devastated by the situation, but still she took her husband back after this happened. She could have been killed, but she felt that her husband completed her image of the perfect life. Teri was misguided and held on at all costs to a fantasy she created in her mind. It wasn't until the relationship became even more volatile that Teri had to let go of her marriage and her story. Through telling herself that she wasn't good enough if she didn't have this husband and the life they built together, Teri allowed her soul to be attacked on a daily basis until she was physically forced to let it go.

Listening to Your Soul

Teri knew things were not right for a long time. She had signs, but ignored her soul crying out for a change. How many times have you felt that something about a person, relationship, job, or situation just wasn't right? How often did you act on that feeling or listen to that intuitive voice? Feelings and instincts are our souls' way of protecting us from spiritual assault. Being able to listen to your inner voice's warnings is our souls' way of saying, "Stop, think, and proceed with extreme caution." Does it matter if our inner voice may be wrong? How bad is it to stop what we are actively doing and think about it before proceeding? It really isn't as long a process as it may seem. If Teri stopped to think about how she was trying to create a man to match the image in the story she created about the perfect couple, she may have seen the flaws in her plan. She would even tell you she never proceeded with caution, even when she jumped on the hood of that moving car.

You will never know for sure if your instincts are right or wrong in the process, but why take a chance? Many times we have gone against our feelings, intuitions, or better judgment, and later wished we hadn't. We often have our souls intuitively speaking to us in many situations. We have learned to listen to that small voice more often than not as we have gotten older.

If we could only tell you how many times it was literally screaming to us, "Don't do that, girl!" and we ignored it and met the outcome with an "I told you so" feeling without anyone having to actually say it. We can't go back and say the outcomes would have definitely been different, but we know that our souls' voices have never led us into danger. Wouldn't you rather be a little more cautious than have something tragic happen that you could have possibly prevented by just being quiet and listening?

We are most susceptible to an assault on our souls when we are weak in mind, feeble in body, and distracted in spirit. Soul predators behave in the same manner as hunters do when they hunt animals. They look for the weak, scared, and easily manipulated. Weakness of mind leaves you open to manipulation. Have you ever known someone who starts out on one side of a debate, but when faced with a master debater ends up on the opposite side? It's one thing to be open to other people's opinions, but it is a whole other thing to be easily swayed from your own. When we don't put in the work to be fully informed about what we are interested in and the world around us, it is so easy to fall prey to someone who wants a doormat to wipe their feet on.

We have met countless women across the country who have expressed how they were victims of mental manipulation. Whether it was a significant other, friend, or family member, they felt hoodwinked. Whenever they expressed these feelings to us we had to ask them what they felt like before they engaged in these manipulative relationships. The common denominator was they felt like victims.

They may not have come out and used the word *victim* or they may just have broken down and said they were victims, but they all felt like victims of one thing or another before they were spiritually attacked. The perceived weakness in their thoughts allowed them to become the victims they were.

Dawn's mom is an ICU nurse. She is the most courageous person we know when it comes to illness. She was at ground zero when the planes hit the towers that morning of September 11th. She tended to the injured and rescue workers. She saw things that were horrifying. People missing limbs, body parts coming in, people disoriented and lost. We didn't know where she was for several hours because she works the night shift and gets off right around the time the first plane hit. She's usually right on the Westside Highway by that time. We were worried and she was right in the thick of it. When she finally did speak to us, she reassured us that she was fine and she would be home when her work was done. That was three days later.

We never thought of Dawn's mother as feeble of body until she was diagnosed with stage 2 ovarian cancer. She was always the authority we went to for medical questions and now she was the patient. The strong, robust woman we knew had to give her job over to others who told her what to do and how to feel. When they say lawyers are their own worst clients, you should see a sick nurse. Feeling helpless in her hospital bed, she said things that were self-defeating. She would talk about her death at times as if it were around the corner just waiting to snatch her up. We all rallied behind her and gave her space to feel the way she felt, but the weakness of her body was changing the way she felt about herself and her life. We knew that if it was one of us who had the cancer she would have been right there saying it was just a bump in the road that we could fix, but since it was her she had her doubts.

You've Got An Attitude!

Yes, we all have an attitude. Our attitude is what allows our souls to be protected or attacked, to live in peace or remain in chaos. It's just as simple as that. Soul predators are usually victims who want to victimize people whom they perceive as weak. You are like a transmitter for anyone who is looking for someone they can spiritually feed off, sometimes unintentionally, but oftentimes not. They look for weak, spiritually helpless victims who are less likely to challenge them and do them harm. Soul predators don't attack the strong of mind and body or the fearless of spirit. They don't want to tangle with anyone who might get the better of them instead.

The key to Soul Survival is attitude. Don't be a victim of mind, body, or a disconnected spirit. Your attitude speaks volumes to people. It is what spiritually attracts others to you. If you have a positive spirit but a weak mind you may attract people who want to manipulate your energy.

They may be looking for an emotional cheerleader, but be

unwilling to reciprocate. If you are strong of mind but weak of spirit you may meet someone who seems your intellectual equal but tries to expose you to things that take you further away from your personal connection to God. Likewise, you may be strong of mind and connected with your soul, but your body may be feeble. Your inability to measure up physically can lead you to doubt yourself and your abilities.

We must fortify ourselves spiritually on all fronts to allow our souls' survival instinct to kick in. There are many times when we are so depleted mentally, physically, and spiritually, it is hard for our souls' voices to be heard through the chaos of life. We had a friend who was in such a space that we were worried that she wouldn't come back from her spiritual assault.

Marissa was a young, vibrant girl who enjoyed life and seemed to have her whole bright future ahead of her. She lived in a great apartment with two roommates and was in a promising career that paid for her education. She was on her way and it seemed like nothing could stop her. She was sent on an assignment that took her out of state for a month. She left the care of her cats to her roommates and only packed the things she needed for her extended trip. When she came home she was exhausted and eager to sleep in her own bed. She never, ever imagined what she came home to—her apartment was abandoned, her clothes and personal belongings were stolen, but more horrifying, her cats were left to starve to death.

She was devastated. Her roommates had her phone number, her family's phone number, and a few close friends' numbers. There was no reason for any of that to have happened. For months Marissa was depressed and despondent and pretty much inconsolable. It wasn't until she was spiritually jolted by an incident that she was able to turn things around and get her life back on track.

Where Do You Live?

It really does matter where you live. Demographics are everything. As businesses prepare to open, they rely on location, location, location. If you buy your first home you research the neighborhood. Check out the schools if you have children. Learn about the crime statistics for the area. Find out how far the nearest market is, or for some of us, the nearest mall. How about climate? East Coast? West Coast? Midwest? North or South?

We take care and time in choosing where we live—that is, if we perceive we have a choice in the matter. What if you have no money to move? What if you grew up in the same little town and no one you knew ever really left? What if you feel trapped in a neighborhood full of drugs and crime? What if all you knew in your life was in a twenty-block radius?

Your state of mind and the state of your soul is very similar—location is everything! Your emotional and spiritual state can determine if you will remain in one place all your life or move to a wonderful place of fulfillment and peace. Like the Jeffersons, you can move on up!

Does your soul live in a neighborhood of doubt, fear, and self-loathing? Your neighbors will tear you down every chance they get, leaving you feeling insecure and depressed. Your soul doesn't care where your physical body is—it really cares where your mind and spirit are. If you are living with these negative thoughts and feelings, you will always feel trapped no matter where you go. You can appear to be on top of the world, but you lean toward self-destructive tendencies. Look at the many young celebrities we see paraded in front of us who seem to have everything anybody would want: money, trips, cars, clothes, jewelry, you name it. So what's wrong? Why do they seem to be doing the same negative things over and over again? They have great physical locations, but their souls are living in bad neighborhoods.

You may be one of those women whose souls grew up in the neighborhood of doubt, anger, and fear, but you managed to move out. But you visit the old neighborhood occasionally because something pops up in life that reminds you of "home." We have experienced this feeling, growing up in seedy neighborhoods with doubt and fear as our neighbors, but with the Grace of God and many spiritual mentors along the way, we have moved to a place of peace with ourselves. There still may come those few occasions when something may be said or done that just takes us back to the old 'hood. Part of our soul revelation is not saying everything is perfect and we are fine, but recognizing the moments that take us back to our old 'hood. Where your soul lives and resides is more important than your physical surroundings. No matter where you live physically, your soul can take you places you have never even imagined or dreamed possible. You can have wonderful neighbors like unconditional love right next door. Trust can be right across the street watching out for you. Sincerity and peace are like the old wise women in your neighborhood that let you know what's going on. And in your very own house is power, faith, and trust.

The funny thing is, you can call up your spiritual realtor today and move in right away. You may be thinking, if it's so simple why hasn't everybody done it yet? It's all about choices. We choose to be where we are, where we are doesn't choose us. Your soul is in the neighborhood it's in because that's your choice. You can't live in both neighborhoods at the same time. You can certainly visit one or the other but you can't reside in both. Where you make your soul's full-time residence is where you will be most of the time. Who doesn't want to live in a nice neighborhood and be looked out for and cared about? It's all about perception. What we perceive as important to us determines where our souls live. Let's go back to the celebs we see self-destructing. They have many influences and pressures that help them determine what is important.

Their perception may oftentimes be formed on the outside and their value placed on things outside of themselves as well. Their spirit becomes so distracted by all the trappings of physical life surrounding them that their perception becomes warped. Latest and greatest party, or peace of mind? You decide. Spiritual distraction is what takes you from your safe, secure neighborhood of peace into doubt, fear, and negativity.

Our good friend Maria Davis can tell you all about where your soul lives and distraction of spirit. She grew up knowing God, but as she became more and more involved in the music industry her focus was placed on her successful MAD Wednesdays Showcase and less on worshipping the Lord. She was caught up in the lifestyle the industry afforded and the people who came in and out of her life that her attention to the Lord waned. In her travels Maria met a handsome man who swept her off her feet, the man she was going to marry. Maria's spirit was always living on the same block with the Lord, but she was distracted and went back to the 'hood. She knew something wasn't quite right, but her focus wasn't on what her soul was trying to tell her: "Let's get out of here and go home!" but on what felt good temporarily. Her spirit was set right when she found out the man she was planning on marrying gave her the AIDS virus. That little visit to the 'hood changed her life. She packed her bags and took her soul right back home. She is doing great and will tell anyone about her journey because it was the lesson she learned that gives her the strength to tell others where their souls need to live.

SOUL REVEALING QUESTIONS

- What are your most vivid memories of growing up?

- How were you treated as a child? Were you treated fairly?

- Is there a history of emotional, physical, or sexual abuse in your family?

- What part of your childhood would you change, given the chance?

- What are your survival techniques?

- Have you received medical attention for mental illness or stress?

- What is your main concern or worry about your life?

- How do you manage your time? Do you find you can do it efficiently? Do you procrastinate or waste time?

- What do you consider to be quality time?

- Have you been in a violent relationship? If so, explain.

Revelations Revealed:

I am a strong, mentally, physically, and spiritually armored warrior. I have the power to protect my soul and listen to its voice intuitively. My soul will always be my guide, helping me to reach my revelations and be the best woman I can be. For my soul, I choose to live in a neighborhood with peace, strength, trust, faith, spiritual security, and unconditional self-love.

Your Revelations Revealed:

CHAPTER 4

The Process of Self-Love

A recent poll found on **Essence.com** states that, "Blacks are now the most unpartnered people in America. Only thirty-four percent of us are married (versus fifty-seven percent of whites), and nearly half of our unions end by the tenth year. Black women are less likely to marry than whites, Hispanics, and even black men." Staggering statistics, but do we consider them shocking? In a society so focused on having a mate, where is the single person researched, examined, or celebrated? How can we create a better communication within ourselves without putting such a great emphasis on partnering?

In our travels and lectures we've found that women of color are more concerned about loving their men than loving themselves. When meeting women we would say to them before signing their books, "Tell us about yourself." Often we would get, "There is nothing to tell," then blank faces and awkward moments of silence. A litany of job titles would follow, like; "I'm a mom," "I'm Jim's wife," "I've been married for ten years," "I'm single," "I'm divorced."

These women were defining themselves based on the relationship they had with other people and not who they were inside. Some confided in us that they did not like their size, hair, and skin color, and then proceeded to give us a wish list of who and what they would like to be. It somehow would include that they wanted to be richer, more outgoing, or wanted to stop living to please others but did not know how. Others had the guts to come right out and say, "I don't like myself."

What gets us to a place of not liking who we are? Or did we ever move out of that place since we were impressionable children? Self-love is very much tied into where your soul lives, as we mentioned in the last chapter, but it takes it a step further. Whenever we talk to women about their relationships we ask them, "Are you attracted to you?" "Do you find yourself sexy and alluring?" "Would you like to marry you?" The emphasis on the man being so fine, sexy, and smart needs to describe yourself. If you aren't attracted to you, why would you expect anyone of quality to be?

How Does Attraction Work?

Physical attraction examines symmetry in facial features and body proportions and can vary among cultures. Being able to look at yourself in the sense of your soul and your ability to like yourself and be attracted to you can also relate to symmetry and proportion. We believe that when there is a symmetry in your thoughts, words, intentions, and actions, you tend to have a balance that leads to self-satisfaction. Having a balanced life is desirable for your soul. You can't think one thing and say another, hoping for a different outcome and act surprised. You wonder what they are talking about? You can't think I want to lose weight, say I don't think I can lose weight, and actually act surprised when the scale doesn't move down a pound or two. Being able to have your thoughts, words, intentions, and actions aligned helps you to lead a happier life and makes you more attractive to you.

Years ago we came across the writings of the distinguished social psychologist Donn Byrne, who had written many journal articles on the theory of attraction. One of the theories that come to mind when we talk about being attracted is the theory of the correlation between reinforcement and attraction. Basically we are attracted to what is reinforced as positive. When we consider someone being attracted to themselves we consider how positive they may feel about spending time alone. There are some people who just can't stand being by themselves, just enjoying their own company. They always seek out the companionship of someone else and wouldn't even consider being alone. How attractive is that?

You like what you like. Try to tease out what it really is that you like about yourself. Are you funny? Do you have great ideas? Do you have sincere feelings? Whatever the special thing or things are about you, self-love is the celebration of those gifts. So many people go through life not really recognizing their true gifts and therefore forgo living to their fullest potential. Or even worse, they know about their gifts, but are too afraid to express them.

I've Been Robbed!

At some point you may have been that confident, self-secure woman who loved yourself and was secure in that feeling. But somehow along the way you were robbed. Dr. Elisabeth Jackson-English, a dear friend and a clinical social worker practicing in New York, explains: "One of the issues of a lack of self-love comes from poor relationships that make a woman feel undesirable, unloved, unappreciated, and unwanted. The roots can be deeply entrenched. It can also stem from a childhood plagued by poor or limited parental guidance and an upbringing supported by alienation and self-doubt."

Some women come from wonderful and loving homes where they were told how smart and beautiful they are from the very beginning. As early as kindergarten you may become exposed to the negative programming other children get from their families. The comments are fast and furious; they will usually start when a child starts exhibiting leadership qualities and talent. It starts off as horseplay, but after hearing, "You think you're all that," or, "You are not that beautiful," or, "Who do you think you are?" it begins to seep into your psyche and make you doubt your abilities.

Candace grew up in a small village in Trinidad in a predominantly poor Indian community. Her parents had migrated to the United States and sent every dollar back home to improve the living conditions of her grandmother, her aunts and uncles, and Candace and her brother. She was taught never to judge anyone and there was no difference between their family and anyone else's. At the age of four she did not understand poverty and the magnitude of it in her village. She thought everyone else had the same things as she and her family. Candace attended a Hindu nursery school in the village. When her classmates came to school without shoes, she wanted to tear off her polished shoes and bright white socks and be barefoot in the heat like her classmates.

One day at lunch she was eating a piece of fruit while sitting on a rock and several of the kids gathered and watched her. No one asked for a piece of her fruit—they just watched as she ate. Upon noticing the attention being diverted from recess the teacher saw what was going on and became enraged. She was so angry with Candace that she screamed at her and told her how selfish she was and then grabbed the fruit from her hands. Candace began to cry as the teacher made her sit on the concrete floor for everyone to stare and frown at her. From that day forward, Candace overgave to the point that it hurt, and her family felt the same way. When they all finally migrated to the United States, her aunts gave away all of her clothes because they felt everyone they were leaving behind in the small village needed them more than they did.

That scenario kept playing out in Candace's life—she was punished for her gifts, both in her personal and professional life. One day, enough was enough. She was offered a great job with a cultural institution and a good friend of hers was her supervisor. She jumped at the opportunity and started getting to work, putting things in order, and really making inroads. Candace really worked hard and people noticed. She never took credit for herself—it was always given to her boss. Everything was going smoothly—that's why it was a shock that after several months of excellent service Candace was fired. When asked why she was let go, she said she was told by her boss, "I couldn't have you here because you are outshining me."

The Road to Self-love

As things take time to manifest in our lives, so does change. Candace experienced a great many challenges, but she also had to begin to examine the role she played in the continuation of her story. The process of self-love is a lifelong journey. But what is really at the root of it? It is, in fact, the trauma hidden deep inside, and as in life our instinct requires some type of scapegoat. It is easier, and even convenient, to blame yourself than examine how you reacted to situations that may have been out of your control.

Life is a circle, and African-American women experience the triple threat of what we call Isim's. We are one of the few races that are devalued, firstly because of our ethnicity, secondly because of our gender, and lastly due to the rise in single-parent homes we have become heads of households with diminishing wealth capacity, leaving us in the bottom portion of the economic scale. When we become victims of crimes, domestic violence, racist or sexist actions, we have no other place to vent our anger and it gets aimed at the closest people to us—our children. It is a concept similar to the spread of an infectious disease—through simple contact the disease of anger passes from one generation to the next, depleting our spirits and ravaging our souls. Eliane Sihera, a writer and

consultant for Diversity Management, Personal Empowerment and Relationships, says, "How do you begin to love
yourself when others might never have affirmed or loved
you? It means you have to try to overturn years of negativity
and being undervalued by parents or lovers."

What Is Your Value?

Do you come first in your own life? How often do you repeat negative affirmations and focus on the downside of your
life? It usually begins with, "I know it won't work," "I don't
want it to fail," or, "Are you sure this will even happen?" With
or sometimes without your conscious knowledge your focus
on the negative increases and then spreads and your results
will be out of line with your intentions. It is all a painful re-
duction of who you are as an individual. You have a significant value to mankind's existence here on earth—how you
choose to execute it is up to you.

Not honoring who you are and the gifts you are able to
contribute to the universe is a disservice to yourself and to
God. Choosing the less-than approach because you feel you
don't deserve more is unacceptable, such as taking less pay
because you are not certain you can do the work, compro-
mising on values with a mate because you don't want to be
alone, or risking not loving someone because it is scary and
you're afraid to be hurt. Fear and self-love cannot coexist. It's
impossible for you to be afraid and continue to give your soul
everything it needs to flourish.

We are taught to look outside of ourselves for reassurance

of our worth. When life feels empty we try to fill the void with things instead of looking at the emptiness and examining the feeling. Voids are usually a result of something being taken away or never existing in the first place. You only recognize it for what it is when you find out you really should have had that experience all along.

It is dysfunctional for us to rely on the ego-driven need for material things to feel "better than most." If you don't love and accept yourself, you are giving your power away and setting yourself up to be a victim. We are trained to be victims and we make this our mantra.

In the *Journal of Examining Depression Among African-American Women from a Psychiatric Mental Health Nursing Perspective* by Barbara Jones Warren, she writes, "I remember one of my clients, a woman who had been brought into the emergency mental health center because she had slashed her wrist while at work. During my assessment, she told me she felt like she was dragging a weight around all of the time, adding, 'I've had all these tests done and they tell me everything is fine physically, but I know it's not. Maybe I am going crazy! Something is terribly wrong with me, but I don't have time for it. I've got a family who depends on me to be strong. I'm the one that everyone turns to.' This woman, more concerned about her family than herself, said she 'felt guilty spending so much time on myself.' When the nurse asked if she had anyone to talk to, she responded, 'I don't want to bother my family and my closest friend is having her own problems right now.' Her comments mirror the sentiments of other depressed African-American women I have seen in my practice. They're alive, but barely, and are continually tired, lonely, and in need."

This sounds like an extreme case, but is it? We all have self-defeating habits and regardless of how few you think they may be, they could quickly snowball. You are priceless and your health and mental well-being should be protected at all cost.

How Well Do You Know Yourself?

Why are women of color in so much pain? Maybe it's because we are constantly confronted with extreme pressure to outperform our counterparts. We are criticized by society as angry and unworthy of love due to the cruel comparisons to women of other ethnic backgrounds. Then sadness settles in due to the objectification and denigration by the men we love. We deal with these situations every day to the point where we don't get to see who we really are as women of color. With all that we are confronted with on a daily basis, it is not hard to believe that we suffer from low self-esteem.

If you have thoughts of being "less than": less important, less attractive, less intelligent, less worthy, you have low self-esteem. Coming to a place of self-love and acceptance will rid you of those feelings and bring you to a place of positive self-image and true self-respect.

Gaining self-confidence in mind and spirit can be a challenge for anyone, but for a woman of color in a society that doesn't honor us it can be a great feat. You may have made a decision to give yourself an attitude adjustment using affirmations and the power of positive thinking, only to find that it didn't work out the way you planned it. If this has happened to you, don't worry—there is hope. As with a diet, it may have taken you a while to gain a lot of weight, and it will take a while to change your perception of yourself. There is no quick-fix diet pill nor is there a quick-fix self-love pill. You can't suddenly change a thought pattern that you have adopted for many years—you will always revert back to the familiar in the beginning. As the saying goes, you need to keep it real. You will have to work hard, maybe harder than you have ever had to work before.

Quitters never win and in the process of learning self-love, there is a winner and a loser and the loser will always be the one who quits before seeing results. Quitting is one of the main reasons we feel the way we feel about ourselves. When your intentions don't match your level of commitment, you lose. You can intend to change, but if you are not willing to put in the work you will never achieve it. Quitters never win and winners never quit. You can't give up on the process when it doesn't feel comfortable. Complaining is a sure sign of quitting. It's so easy to complain about your feelings but it is harder to restrain from the pity party and actually do something about it.

Now that we have gotten past the pity and regret, we can get down to business. Instead of looking for your friends to affirm you, you need to be your own number one cheerleader. Cheer yourself on and don't wait for praise—it will come, but you have to earn it. Our friend Tiffany is a firm believer in this concept. She's quick to tell anyone she can't rely on others for her happiness. She wakes up with the attitude that she's the master of her universe and with God she knows anything is possible. "Any woman can feel that way if she believes it. I have done some crazy things, and other women would just say, 'Wow, I can't believe you did that.' I know who I am and what I want and I go for it.

"Every woman of color needs to look in the mirror and tell herself that she is beautiful, powerful, and deserves to be happy—and feel confident, successful, and sexy. I do it every day. It's not conceit, it's confirmation. I have created that feeling within myself, so when someone wants to tear it down because I won't conform to their desires, I am ready," Tiffany says. "Being your own personal cheerleader and best friend allows you to create the relationship you desire with yourself. It creates your safe place so you can be reenergized with faith and love every day. We are best friends, but when we need a kind word, the other may not always be available—that's why we need to create those kind words within ourselves as do you.

"Make your next move your best move. I never compare myself to anyone else because I'm unique and so are you," says Tiffany. "We all have gifts and we need to utilize them to the best of our abilities." As Tiffany lectures about self-esteem and dating, she says, "Stay in your lane and know your market. We all have our 'thing' and whatever your 'thing' is, own it and make it work for you. Take pride in who you are and recognize that you are special and use it to your advantage. You are like no other and you need to realize that. Why would you want to be me, and likewise, why would I want to be you?

There is enough room for everyone, and we can't believe we have limits," says Tiffany. "Everything will fall into place once you get on board your own train. You will see the difference in the way people treat you."

Tiffany adds, "A smile goes a long way. Never let them see you frown because you know where your happiness lies. I definitely believe in treating every impression as if it were the first. There will come times when you feel down, but it is temporary and not worth dwelling on. Remain positive and keep the focus on the things you are grateful for all the time," she believes. "Lastly, things happen. When you remain confident and positive within yourself, you have no option but to know you deserve the best life has to offer. Never settle for less and you will never receive less. We are all capable of greatness and I know deep down inside you know it, too!"

The Past Is Now

The great thing about making mistakes is that you learn from them. If you are willing to be open and honest with yourself you can learn a great deal about how to move forward. So many people lie to themselves about their mistakes or are just so ashamed they can't examine them. Mistakes are God's way of telling us we need to reevaluate our positions. The great part about it is the past is now. If you have just read this, it's past. You can take comfort from the fact that whatever you are beating yourself up about or denying is in the past. You can make a change right now. You can forgive yourself first, and then examine what it is that you need to do next time. Or, you can stop lying to yourself and say, "Okay, I made a mistake and now it's over." Yes, some mistakes are bigger than others, and yes again, some mistakes alter lives, but it's never too late for change. As women of color we are sometimes harder on ourselves than anyone else can be. It's time to say, I forgive me. I am ready to move on to a place of self-love and total acceptance. Repeat it as often as possible with sincerity and conviction. Take it in, believing it is so, and allow it to seep into your soul.

Looking Into the Future

Having a great outlook for the future helps you change your current perception of yourself. As you work at revealing your soul and loving yourself, you will be ready for positive change and self-love.

Being Thankful:

Are you grateful for some of the things that are in your life that we take for granted? The fact that you woke up this morning and have another wonderful day to do something is exceptional. Take stock of your life, the beauty that appears each day, the moments that go unnoticed, the wonderful people who are willing to be helpful, the talent that comes so easily, the children who are a part of your life, even if you did not have them physically. They are here to teach you valuable lessons and you are to sow into them the seeds of hope. How

...he numerous opportunities bestowed upon you even if ...were not prepared for them? Is there an element of ...nkfulness incorporated into your life each and every day?

What Is Your Life's Passion?:

Are you following your true passion in life? What excites you and makes you happy just to think about it? Clarifying how you want to spend the rest of your life is important in order to expand your life's mission. Your passion is fun, comes from the heart—it is that fire in your belly that engages you and is not difficult to pursue. If you would be happier following your life purpose, then why are you living a life of less-than? If you are honest with yourself, you can create the result that you really want. Janet Bray Attwood and Chris Attwood's Passion Test (www.healthywealthynwise.com) will help you identify your markers and set you on your path.

Self-actualization and Appreciation of Self:

You are a beautiful woman and how you came to be here on earth is a miracle in itself. Accept who you are—your body, limitations, abilities, gifts, and character flaws—they are all elements of who you are. It is unnatural to seek perfection. Most perfectionists are unable to accomplish major goals because they are stuck on the small things. There is not one human being in the world who is perfect. Perfection is unattainable, but doing your very best in every circumstance of your life is possible. Minimize the good old I "should have and could have" conversation and recognize what you can do differently in the future and add this to your arsenal of information. That includes living for the present and leaving the past behind. Do you accept yourself for exactly who and what you are? You have been given an amazing talent and gift by God and He is ready, willing, and able to increase your abundance. Your gift is unique to you and it was designed to enhance the lives of others. What is your gift and are you ready to share it?

Self-forgiveness:

You have to let go of the past. Easier said than done, but it is necessary to start the healing process. Have you ever spoken with a friend or loved one who, when they start repeating an incident, their voice becomes higher and their body tenses up as if they are reliving the situation all over again? Your mind and body are really not aware that you are not actually going through this trauma; we call it *repeat and relive.* When you have been traumatized, you repeat the story maybe a dozen times to friends and loved ones. Each time you repeat and relive, your body goes into stress mode, releasing hormones as if you were going through it the very first time. It is your way of punishing yourself and as the experience becomes overwhelming, it brings forth your anxiety. Get the story out and keep it out. Refrain and renew—look for a new beginning within the context of the situation.

African-American women also have a tendency to wear their troubles as badges of honor. Somehow it feels comforting to control your disappointments and live your life just being okay. These are self-destructive patterns and practices which we inadvertently use as attention-getters because of the great need to have someone recognize that we are hurt. In actuality, it has the opposite effect and alienates people. No one wants to be part of your constant rainy day.

You need to forgive yourself for any misdeeds. Accept the responsibility and move on. The only way to grow and accept love in your life is to release the pain from previous situations. It will take a leap of faith, sometimes even changing your demographic location, as Charise Johnson found as she tells us her story.

"Years earlier, in college, my girlfriends and I had strolled the perimeter of raucous party-crowds, proudly rep'ing our hometown . . . *'When I say Little, you say Rock . . . Little . . . ROCK! Little . . . ROCK!'* with at least as much arrogance and verve as the sorority girls had for their red-and-white, pink-and-green, blue-and-white alliances. That day, the very city which had claimed its place in history by mustering armed forces to escort nine black students to educational freedom was the very same prison from which I so desperately needed to escape. No matter where I went, there I was . . . his former wife, her ex-daughter-in-law, his brother's ex-wife, and his baby-mama . . . Where had the former *me* run off to?

"I'd left my husband.

"I'd heard folks refer to divorce as if it were a first cousin to Death . . . a tragic, emotion-soaked loss of a loved one, complete with the change of address, perfunctory expressions of sympathy, and financial strain, but with no gravesite . . . no monument to the marriage that used to be. I'd heard my grandmother say, 'Nobody gets married to get divorced, baby.' Her simple, straightforward wisdom grated on my threadbare nerves as I packed the last of my son's toys and scrawled

'Zachary' on the cardboard box. *Maybe they do, Grand-mamma.*

"I chose Dallas, Texas.

"In a city with five million people and traffic that would test the patience of Job, I felt a bit alienated initially. Mama wasn't ten minutes away anymore. I was no longer the carefree, size-two ingénue I'd been before I married, gave birth, and divorced a man I still liked, but no longer loved. Invitations to happy hours and swanky soirees were supplanted by preschool parties and play dates. Fridays were Blockbuster nights, Saturdays were for grocery shopping and the park . . . we were both learning to ride without training wheels. I was only receptive to the romantic advances of men from out of town, and my house was off-limits to them when my son was home. I asked God to take away my desire for a relationship, the way He'd done for the Apostle Paul. Thus far, He's done no such thing, but He has kept me and my little boy safe and blessed us to be happy. He helped me to find my former self, and even upgraded her somewhat in spirit, faith, self-reliance, and determination.

"I am who I thought I was.

"Yes, to some I am still her ex-daughter-in-law, her man's ex-wife, blah, blah, blah . . . But to my son I am Mom. To me, I am strong, funny, resourceful, smart, and yes, cute. To God I am exceptional. And because of Him, I am healed."

Chances are if you have spent some time in your skin you have to look around and come to an understanding that if you don't like you, or you can't stand being with yourself, not by yourself, how can you expect someone else to want to be with you? Self-love is a power source that provides a critical tool to provide the strength to help you overcome your fears and doubts. Dr. English believes that self-appreciation, self-forgiveness, and gratitude are also necessary and need to be put in place to begin on the path to regain our self-love. "As women we need to live in the present and stop dwelling on the past and our ancestors' beliefs."

In a poll published in the 2006 journal *Race, Gender and Class*, conducted by researchers Professor Ashraf Esmail and Assistant Professor Jas M. Sullivan, ninety-six percent of the men preferred a medium-to-light complexion in women while seventy percent of women found light skin of value in men. This was taken from a sampling of fifty African-American men and fifty African-American women students at a mid-western University.

The analysis of mating preferences explored a number of probable causes, all of which were rooted in the "colorism" from slavery and social stigma through the 1960s, when lighter skin typically meant more privilege.

The women who participated in the study took into account characteristics such as a man's lips, hair, eyes, height, and style of dress when determining his attractiveness.

One student pointed out, "I think that people are valued for their light skin. You can take this theory way back to the house-slave mentality. Since that was valued, a lot of people were taught to value light skin. It is still ongoing—society has not lost that altogether."

Both men and women cited media as the key influence in the preference for lighter skin. One woman participant stated, "When you talk to a guy, he thinks he wants the perfect girl he sees on the videos. Usually, the women portrayed in the videos are light-skinned and have long hair."

Sometimes the news perpetuates this ideal as with Don Imus, a former host of a national Sports Talks show simulcast on television and radio. He called members of the Rutgers women's team "nappy-headed hoes," and was dismissed as a result.

We must be outraged when incidents like this happen, especially since we are responsible for paving the way for ourselves and all the women who come after us as did the women before us.

A New York City mother and grandmother, Sylvia Ancrum, stated, "Imus is one of a slew of radio personalities (these so-called, 'shock jocks') who need to be censored. They divulge too much information to our children, including foul language and insults. As sisters of color, and maybe a few brothers as well, we must unite to say no to this and any other kind of rhetoric that degrades women, regardless of their race."

Actually, when we did *Souls of My Sisters* we felt the book would be a tool to heal women as each generation is judged by their music. If you or your relatives lived through these times, you have your own personal anthems. The 50s was the era of big band and sugary songs of love and promise, and on the fringes was the emergence of R&B, Rock, and Jazz; the 60s gave us a full-scale Rock and Roll and R&B that made us joyous; the 70s vivid anti-war songs and shouts of I am black and proud; the end of the 80s, 90s, and beginning of the twenty-first century simply scare us.

We wanted our children and their children to have a body

of work that showcased the strength and beauty of black women and not resort to reciting the words to songs and literature that called us bitches or hoes or how we got pimped with our baby mama drama.

Regardless of the circumstance, even local musicians are cashing in all the way to the bank by degrading black women. It does not mean that you have to incorporate this into your value systems. Appreciate all your accomplishments and achievements.

"It is also critical for us to forgive ourselves for our mistakes and use each and every day as an opportunity to improve our shortcomings. Today, just forgive your poor choices in relationships, marriages, employment decisions and let it go," states Dr. Elisabeth Jackson-English. "We also need to thank God for good health, and the health of our family and friends, all our faculties and senses, for merely seeing another day to make a change and to experience love. We aren't thankful enough for what has been placed in our lives. For some godforsaken reason, we can't seem to give thanks and demonstrate appreciation for these things—if we didn't have them we would really be in trouble!"

It is absolutely necessary to give yourself the respect, consideration, and love you deserve. Your core self-esteem concerns every aspect of your life: your realism, rationality, and independence. Poor self-esteem correlates directly with irrationality, fear, defensiveness, hostility, and controlling behavior. Life has a natural ebb and flow—you need to take your experiences and allow them to make you stronger.

SOUL REVEALING QUESTIONS

● What are you holding on to that you believe needs to be healed?

● What issues in your past are of particular concern to you? Are you comfortable sharing your past experiences with others?

● Do you use drugs or alcohol? How does that impact the relationships you have with others?

● How comfortable are you with your body?

● What pattern would you need to incorporate in your life to improve your health?

● Describe your closest friends. Are you just like them or do you want to be like them?

● How vulnerable are you to pressure from your peers?

● How much do you rely on your friends' opinions?

Revelations Revealed:

How do you resist the temptation not to love yourself? With the first hint of rejection, some of us immediately

*throw our hands up and give in. What we fail to real-
ize is that regaining self-love is a process. Ultimately
the process of self-love begins with the mind. Continue
to work each day on clearing all self-defeating words
out of your vocabulary as well as the people who per-
petrate it. Become a spiritual warrior—set yourself
free from the burden of self-doubt using Bible power.*

Your Revelations Revealed:

CHAPTER 5

Standing in the Gap
of Grace

Change is hard and realization is even harder. Sometimes when we are trying to create positive changes in our lives, the people around us resist. They become critical and judgmental, especially if the change we are trying to make affects our relationship with them. How do we continue on our journey when we are confronted with roadblocks, the loss of our cheerleading squad, obstacles, and outright rebellion? Being responsible for our reaction to life and its experiences is part of the process. Being confident that we can make a difference and living for our life's purpose is the gap between staying in a state of life support and achieving the truth of the revelation that God has for us. How do we stand in the gap of grace and move forward to the true gift?

Most people go through things that bring them to the brink, forcing them to build a bridge over that gap and into grace. They call it vicissitudes, or the changing fortunes of life. We have all said it: "If I was five minutes ahead of myself, or a couple more inches that would have been it." We can admit it gets tough when life comes at us with the unexpected. And if we choose to live in denial, it can eat away at our soul and destroy us emotionally.

A boyfriend hatching a master plan to leave you in the most hurtful way; an employer turning you into a scapegoat for something that you warned him/her about repeatedly months before; a close-knit family fighting during the planning of a funeral after a sudden death of a relative; teens acting up against your rules because you want the best for them but they believe they know more than you; friends saying and doing hurtful things when you no longer can be there for them; helping others who really just want to waste your time and not help themselves—these are all experiences that can sap your energy and dampen your spirit. We know firsthand because these things have happened to us.

During such times, all you can say is, it hurts. It hurts from every angle of your soul. You question, "What brings this chaos in my life and how have I contributed to it?"

Chaos is defined as "a condition or place of great disorder or confusion." When you add chaos to your life it's hard to figure out exactly what's happening. Things are out of your control. Time seems to move too fast, and you feel trapped. But chaos can be organized. Take a step outside the chaos. Figure out the root of the chaos and address it as rationally and logically as possible until you're back on track.

During chaotic times you have no choice but to rely on self-love and lean on God. Sometimes you may also rely on others, people whom God has placed in your path to help you on your journey—a journey He planned a long time ago for you.

Pamm Malveaux's Story

"When I look back at that tumultuous time in my life, I thank God for teaching me about unconditional self-love and compassion. I often hear God whisper in my soul, 'I AM THE LORD. I control all things. Before you were formed I knew you, Pamm, and now I have come to answer your prayers. I really will.' God loves me so much and truly desires the best for my life. He takes great joy in seeing me live a life of victory. Be encouraged—you, too, are a child of the most high.

"Recently, *Souls of My Sisters* would once again stand in the gap of grace with me. It was the day after the video shoot for this book. I suddenly had to rush my mother to the hospital—she was dying in my arms. Oh my God, have mercy on me! I needed her. I wasn't ready to see her go and her tears told me she wasn't, either. Suddenly my phone rang. It was Candace Sandy. Our scheduled conference call would become a powerful prayer session with my sister, Tracy, that kept my mother alive until the paramedics arrived! Praise the Lord! Oh my Soul, the words of Maria Davis: 'Death is not an option!' Thank you, Candace and Maria, for standing in the gap of grace!

"My *Souls of My Sisters* would continue to stand in the gap of grace for me during that long week when my mother was in the hospital, during which my family turned against me, thinking I was trying to kill my mother . . . prayers, calls, and e-mails from Candace and Maria reminded me that I AM THAT I AM! My tears were their tears . . . our tears. I realized that I was and will always be one with my sisters.

"I will always remember that when life gets hectic, I will take the time to seek the inner pocket—EVEN WHEN I CAN'T FIND SOMEONE TO STAND IN THE GAP OF GRACE FOR

ME! I know God will always give me the answer with the question."

Leading Under Adversity

The gap can sometimes be filled with roadblocks that we need to overcome. Leading under adversity requires a balance of work and personal life, persistence, focus, and optimism. But what happens when, in an attempt to overcome the obstacles, our perception is tainted? There is a fine line between optimism and denial. When you are optimistic about a situation, you can focus on a positive outcome, but when you are in denial, the outcome is inevitable and there is nothing you can do to change it. But sometimes it is a struggle to remain optimistic, especially in the face of grief—as Shelley Roxanne discovered.

Shelley Roxanne's Story

"'I'm sorry, she's gone,' he says. I'm sorry? Are you kidding me? Is that all you can say? I don't remember his name, not sure if I ever knew it, but I will never forget his face, as he was the man who pronounced her dead. It seemed so final, so permanent, so irrevocable. Who would pick such a job? The job of having to tell loved ones that someone they loved so dearly has . . . expired. But this is my mother, the woman who brought me into this world, my girlfriend, my biggest fan, my entire support system, and yet here in this cold emergency room lies the lifeless body of a beautiful angel, someone I'm not sure is my mother. Because my mother is full of life—vibrant, powerful, strong, and beautiful.

"She would never leave me here to fend for myself alone. Fear, pain, confusion, anger, and hurt are just a few of the hundreds of emotions I felt at that very second; and as the weeks and months went by, I would feel them over and over again, at differing points throughout the day.

"Mom always used to tell me, 'Write it down. When you experience something joyful or painful, write it down.' What was it with her and documentation? She always encouraged me and her grandchildren, my sons, to write. Maybe she knew how cathartic this process would be.

"It has actually taken me months to put pen to paper and write how I feel about this life-changing experience. Yes, I did a radio show and talked in front of millions about it, but I hadn't yet done what she recommended, and that was to write about it—at least not until now.

"A motherless child, an orphan—that's how I felt then and sometimes on rainy days I still do. Ironically, just one month after the sudden passing of my best friend, my mother, my Glo, I was named a 2007 Woman of Influence by a national magazine. What timing, I thought. I was confronted with the fact that I have spent my life encouraging people to be optimistic about the future and yet here I am, not sure how to do that myself. But this is an amazing honor, and Glo would be thrilled, right?

"The emotions I felt when I opened that magazine to the two-page spread with a huge picture of me and the attached article headed with 'The Best is Yet to Come' are hard to explain, even now.

"Those are my words, I thought, and the message from Glo was so very clear. She reminded me of my life's work. Reminded me of one of the 10 Commandments of Optimistic Living (c) I developed days before she passed away. Commandment #5 says: Thou shall give what you need—give to others the thing(s) you need most in your life, be it forgiveness, time, money, love, friendship, or even encouragement. Whatever you give comes back to you—multiplied. And so, I gave encouragement to others because that is what I needed most at that time, and frankly, still do.

"Ironically, the photo used in the magazine was taken the last night I saw my mother alive. I look so much like her. My son Evan said the picture looks as if Nana and I have morphed into one and the same person. Can that be true? I know we all become like our mothers as we grow up, but is it more than that? Maybe Evan is right. I stared at this photo of me/Glo and I thought—WOW. Wow is all I could say as I welled up with tears. Glo would be so proud right now, I thought. I quickly called my father. Surely he will scream with joy and beam with pride to see his baby girl in a national magazine. 'Come right over, Dad, I have something to show you that you will be so excited to see,' I said. Hey, was I just telling him how he should feel or what? (That is such a Glo thing to do.) Anyway, a few hours later my dad gets to my house. The door opens and my excitement is nearly uncontrollable at this point but I do hold it in. I hand him the magazine, hoping he will flip to the right page. He slowly passes through the magazine as I'm thinking, what is taking him so long? I urge him, 'Turn to page 28-29!' He ignores the advice, eventually getting to the page anyway.

"Okay, I thought, here it comes; here come the screams, the jumping with joy and pride! But instead, guess what he did—none of the above. He closed the magazine and began talking to one of my sons about his day. Man, are you crazy? Don't you see me standing here feeling like a five-year-old girl who has just brought home her first piece of artwork from kindergarten? Don't you see me in desperate need of a Glo scream or cackle of laughter right now? But then it hit me— I was being unfair to this man. My father's reaction is the very same one he would have given me prior to January 6, 2007.

"It was at that moment that I realized I was looking for a Glo reaction from my father. Don't get me wrong, he eventually said it was nice and gave me that megawatt smile that said 'I'm proud of you,' but I realized then that I never noticed how he was because he was always a part of a 'they.'

"They included Mom and Dad, my parents, the 'them' in my life who had been lovers, friends, and partners for 57 years. I always referred to 'them' as one. I even had the audacity to tell him—respectfully, of course—that unlike his lackluster reaction, Glo would have been so proud and excited right now. 'Yes, she would,' he said. 'Yes, she would.'" And he walked out my door. Well, you're a big girl now, Shelley Roxanne. Your lead cheerleader is not here, at least not in the same way she was before, so you had better learn how to cheer for yourself. After all, you and Glo are now one, so let the Glo in you give you the cheers and accolades you need at times like these. I have taken the best of Glo and the best of me and decided to merge them into one powerful woman. Watch out, world, Glo's baby girl is all grown up and confident that the best really is yet to come."

Our life lessons start and end with self, though along the way you will have loved ones helping and guiding you on the magnificent journey. Ultimately they will be showing you how to depend on yourself, love yourself, and trust yourself.

It's Time to Clean House

We accumulate so much in our lives. Walking around our neighborhoods in the spring and summer there are sidewalk and garage sales. Most of what we collect we never use. The urge to posses the item was greater than its utility. Some of these items were put in a closet and never saw the light of day until the sidewalk sale. We all do it—clothing, shoes, purses, items that just don't fit in our homes, but they take up space. Our homes, closets, purses, minds, and lives are cluttered and God keeps giving us clues that it is time to clean house. Getting rid of things—and even people—that have cluttered your space to make room for optimism and hope is difficult. What will you do with all this stuff? How can you clean house and create space for you?

In the middle of adversity it becomes clear who you will need to remove from your life. Like a severely messy apartment, you and only you will know when you have had enough. It was obvious before, but sometimes we need a thump in the head. The number one reason why we do not include more people who are positive and moving in a direction that we would like to go is that we are intimidated by them, and we have self-defeating habits deeply embedded in our lives. Incorporating positive people in your life will boost your energy and create an equal exchange of support and friendship.

Soul Emergency Readiness Kit (SERK)

The United States Homeland Security has an emergency readiness plan called Ready America that says prepare, plan, and stay informed in case of a disaster or terrorism. We believe that your Soul's Emergency Readiness Kit shouldn't be that different. When you are standing in the gap of grace you need all the tools in your soul's survival kit to help you. Here are the tools you will need:

Flashlight—The flashlight in your kit is your intuition that helps to illuminate your way as you are trying to cross the valley between your current state and a state of grace. Your intuition leads you to where you need to be in the darkness of crisis.

Fresh Water—Your soul's fresh water is the replenishment it needs from positive words of hope and faith. Your Bible and other positive texts let you know by faith that anything is possible.

Radio—Your radio provides much needed information from professionals who may have been where you are and can tell you how they were able to get through the crisis.

Food—Fresh food nourishes your body as fresh thoughts and positive thinking nourish your soul. You need spiritual nutrients to survive in the gap and to be able to get to the other side.

Dust Mask—You need something to help you filter out all the advice and opinions you will receive while you are crossing the gap. Not all advice is good—you need to be able to listen to people's opinions objectively and decide what is best for you.

The basics in your soul's survival kit will get you through the gap and help protect and guide you on your way to grace.

Gaining Ground in the Gap

Your best help in removing the biggest roadblock in the gap of grace—YOU—starts with implementing key strategies for change. We subscribe to the notion that, "Tactics without strategy is the noise before defeat," as quoted by warrior Sun Tzu, in *The Art of War.* You actually need to become a warrior to create and defend the purpose of your life. Find new methods to remain focused while in the center of the storm and follow up faithfully.

It is easy to live life or have life live you, but a person who can stand in the gap of grace stands with fortitude and purpose. When you are clear about your life's mission, nothing can deter you.

Another key strategy for dealing with adversity is to reexamine how you have chosen to deal with stress. Prayers and meditation are critical tools that give you the opportunity to spend time with God and clear your mind so you can go about the business of completing your mission here on this earth. God will walk with you and if you become tired He will carry you, but only if you let Him.

In the middle of adversity the aggressor is seeking to make you angry, priming you for defeat. Anger serves as a distraction and is used to keep you off track. Neutralize your aggressor by not reacting. It will stump and bewilder them, but it gives you time to examine the issue and sort through it while asking yourself what this is really about.

SOUL REVEALING QUESTIONS

- Have you experienced being attacked at a critical point in your life?

- How did you feel during and after that experience?

- Did you abandon your dream?

- What lesson did you learn about yourself?

- How much time do you spend working? Is it often during evenings, days off, weekends and holidays?

- Who did you surround yourself with during tough times—cheerleaders or naysayers?

- Were you able to focus on the light at the end of the tunnel? Or were you in a fog?

- How do you think it prepared you for your next life crisis?

- Give an example of leading under adversity.

- Are you a spontaneous person or do you need to plan your time based on a schedule?

- What do you consider to be quality time?

- What is your typical day like?

- How can you eliminate chaos from your life?

Provide five ways in which you can seed optimism in your life.

a)

b)

c)

d)

e)

Revelations Revealed:
Road blocks will not deter me and fear will not prevent me from living my life in God's grace in a perfect way.

Your Revelations Revealed:

CHAPTER 6

Spiritual Awakening

Have you ever been tired? It is almost a restless feeling; you are exhausted mentally and physically, and you just don't have room for one more thing. You have had enough of everything and just need to stop the madness. If you are tired or have been tired, you are on your way to your very own spiritual awakening. What you have done in the past just isn't working for you anymore.

Being tired and giving up are two totally different things. Being tired is the exhaustion you will feel before your breakthrough. You must get to a space where you are ready and totally committed to change. It can't be halfway. I have come to this state many times and it was my catalyst for change— changing what I was doing and taking a step back to examine what I could do better. It's the "To thine own self be true" way of thinking. If you can't take the time to stop and be honest with yourself, who can you expect to be honest with you?

Who Am I?

In *Souls of My Sisters* we discussed "Woman in the Mirror." We asked: When you look in the mirror, who do you see? A woman of substance, beauty, intelligence? Do you see yourself as healthy and able? Do you see truth, or do you see lies? Are you still living a story that causes self-hatred and shame? Instead of cooperating actively in our lives, we are so busy doing everything possible to be distracted from what is important, limiting our success and reducing our happiness.

How did you get here? How did you get to this space in your life? Chart out how you were able to get into the space you are in right now. What were the disappointments? What were the successes? Which patterns have kept reoccurring? What really hurts? What are you really interested in working on? The litany of questions may have your head spinning, but we are so busy in our everyday lives that we don't take the time to do the introspective work necessary for the care of our souls.

Self Inquiry

Looking inside yourself is critical to finding out who you are. Sometimes this can be very difficult because you need to be totally honest. No half-stepping. Unplug the phone, turn off the television, go offline, and give yourself a clear space. Think about the type of person you are at this moment (not who you were or who you strive to be). What turns you on, what are your passions, what are your weaknesses, what are your strengths? How do you feel about the world around you? How do you relate to others? Can you relate to yourself—are you in tune with your needs, in tune with your body, in tune with your thoughts? If it helps, act like you are about to interview yourself. Write down a list of probing, personal questions, then answer them.

You Are Special

We are nurtured as children to believe we are special and then the world tells us otherwise. Some of us didn't even have the benefit of being told by our parents that we were worthy or special. Everyone is special. No one thinks like you, acts like you, or has the same exact desires as you. You are a unique individual—and it's time to celebrate that fact. Be your own person; don't always try to blend into a crowd. When you try to adapt wholly to others you lose yourself. You are not being honest about your own feelings, opinions, and powers. It's okay to be special. Sometimes others try to knock you down—they do so not only because they are intimated by your confidence, but because they themselves are afraid to be themselves, afraid to be special. Don't let someone else's angst cause you to downplay who you are. As the saying goes, "It's their problem, not yours." Revel in just how special you are!

Release judgment of yourself and others and accept the abundance of blessings God has in store for you. Hold your head up high because God don't make no junk. It's time to set aside your preconceived notions about others and even about yourself. Once you let go of the human tendency to pass judgment, you will open yourself up to new experiences and self-acceptance. There will be wonderful surprises, learning experiences, new opportunities. Passing judgment on others—and yourself—is a cop-out. It's taking the easy road and not focusing on why you feel inadequate.

If you make up your mind before an experience, then you don't have to be challenged. But think of the growth that comes with challenges. This doesn't mean you have to compromise yourself or your values—it just means to step out of your box while still maintaining who you are. Take food for a simple example. Just because you think you won't like Indian food, you don't try it. But wait a minute. What happens if you dare to taste an Indian dish—and you love it! That's something new to excite your taste buds, to open your palate, to add to your menu. Now look at life in this way. There are new people, new experiences just waiting for you.

What is greater than you? You know there is something out there greater than you. It is as if there was some type of plastic film wrapped around your life and all you need to do is break through. How can you build your faith, as exercise would help you to build your physical strength and endurance? Awakening your spirit is submitting to the Lord's will and eliminating anything that holds you back and doesn't fit in His plan. That means refusing to partake of anything that would compromise your values and spirit. Regardless of how good it feels. Do you trust God. Some question the existence of God, but think how hard it must be to believe that the weight of the world is literally on your shoulders. To have nothing greater than yourself in your life to submit to or give your burdens to is a lonely and worrisome position to be in. The anxiety and angst build up, and yes, you can tell a friend, but they can't work it out for you, either. The reliance on something greater than yourself is what helps to alleviate the burdens and allows us to be the best we can be at any given moment.

Getting to Your Revelation Moment

Your spiritual awakening is that proverbial tipping point that can go either way and is the moment before the acceptance of your awakening. These moments are more frequent than you may expect—it's just that so many of us get there but we revert to old habits instead of accepting the truth of the revelation. It is a change in how you look at things and a defining moment of true understanding. The shift in your thinking usually causes changes to occur in your entire life. We've witnessed true faith through the experiences the women faced in *Souls of My Sisters*. Their faith was demonstrated through their spiritual awakening. It was that inspirational epiphany, the sudden clarity, the small voice that guided them to do what they needed to do regardless of the challenges set before them.

When we first approached some of the women in *Souls of*

My Sisters, they balked at the fact that we were asking them to talk about some of their deepest secrets. These were issues that they themselves may not have fully dealt with. When they started attending the workshops and book signings, they thought they were there to share their stories. Instead, it became an equal exchange, a collective healing opportunity for all parties involved. Most of all, they each found a way to tap into that source deep inside themselves when they needed it most, but they always praised God even in the quiet, peaceful times as well as in the darkness of their struggle.

Our faith in God and the awakening of our spirit became the collective core of our foundation; it has sustained us, opened doors, and given opportunity even when things seemed bleak. In the midst of dealing with the pain of each of their stories, God sanctioned their missions. The women saw a need in each of their lives and started getting to work. They were not concerned whether they were qualified or where the funding would come from. It was as if God just said, "Here you go—this is your mission," and they were off and running.

The missions were varied, like Maria Davis, who told her story about HIV/AIDS and became a national spokesperson for Bristol Myers Squibb, BET's Wrap It Up Campaign, and still has the energy to crisscross the country to participate in hundreds of events about HIV/AIDS every year. Deacon Patti Webster and her mother, Reverend Patricia Webster, who started the Real to Reel Conference where each year in New Jersey they minister to women who fly in from across the country to hear God's word. Darnelle McCullough started the

Mama, Are You Scarred Angel Wings project that focuses on working with young people whose parents have been afflicted with or died from HIV/AIDS. These are just a few examples of the many things these women have accomplished and continue to do with the help of His guidance and grace.

God planted a seed of purpose in each one of the contributors in *Souls of My Sisters,* just as He has planted a seed within you. It is what you do to nurture that seed that counts. When you are clear about what God's assignment for your life is, everything will fall into place. It becomes almost easy to make decisions, and there are no conflicts or hard feelings when you know that it is God's plan you are implementing and nothing else matters.

When someone commented that his political setback was a blessing in disguise, Winston Churchill replied, "Damn good disguise." Believing that God has unprecedented favor in your life and all things have a divine order will set you on a path to prosperity. God is expressing His will through your life, so opportunities will appear. Your spirit will awaken, your intuition will be heightened, and your ability to make decisions will be clear and concise. And the very best life of God's life in you will be fulfilled.

Obedience to His will also means surrendering. The Bible states: be anxious for nothing, but in everything by prayer and supplication, with thanksgiving, let your requests be made known to God; and the peace of God, which surpasses all understanding, will guard your hearts and minds through Christ Jesus. (Philippians 4:6-7)

It's Time to Clean House

Getting rid of the clutter in your life is critical to your spiritual awakening. Ever hear someone say that a cluttered desk is a cluttered mind? When you have too much clutter in your life, it's hard to think clearly. You're bogged down by minutia. So clear it out!

What is clutter? Clutter can be anything that is a jumbled collection, whether it be in your physical space or in your mind. Are you thinking too much about everything? Then that's clutter. Hold in your mind only what is important, what truly matters. Clear your space, keeping only the things you need and cherish. Do you have a clutter of people surrounding you? End the toxic relationships and even some of those that are not in order to promote your spiritual awakening. Surround yourself with people who don't clutter you with their tales of woe. Once you've made space physically and mentally, you will open the door for new blessings and opportunities to arrive.

God's Provision

In *Souls of My Sisters* we have a technique that works for us—Prayerfection, which we use to be more focused on inner peace. It allows you to find a space that is quiet so that you can concentrate on your prayers. We take time away from our lives to write, meditate, and pray. You can pray anywhere, creating that silence in your mind and soul to connect with God. We have prayed in the bathroom, in the middle of Times Square, and even at a concert. You can pray and communicate with God all day long, but you also need spiritual retreat time where there is nothing but you and God. We all need a special place, a weekend retreat—take one day a month and head out to the beach, lake, park, or library for a few hours. If you are at home, surround yourself with comforting items like flowers and candles. Release your spirit and have a conversation with God.

Record your dreams each morning, as they may have even greater meaning in your subconscious thought patterns. Keep a journal of your story. Record your thoughts on whatever comes to mind. Begin to fortify your relationship with God and incorporate quiet time for a peaceful resolution. Reassess the decisions you have made or just simply rest your mind. Use the time to write in *Souls Revealed* to gather your thoughts. This simple time away from your life will give you an opportunity to put things in perspective. "There is not a day that passes that I do not stand in remembrance of how I got over. My soul does not have to look back and wonder how I got over," states Oprah Winfrey. "This I know for sure—God can dream a bigger dream for you than you can ever dream for yourself!"

Making Every Moment in Your Life Count

Time is swift. A week can disappear without you even remembering what happened. If this is how you are going through life, you are missing out on the precious moments that help shape you. It takes effort not to get caught up in the rat race, but it is so worth it to take time to smell the roses. Even if you are strapped for time, at the end of the day take a moment to reflect on the day's events—even if you have to lock yourself in the bathroom to get away from the hubby and kids. It is important to look back at your day. Think about what you accomplished, what you didn't get to do, conversations you had, new things/people you saw. How was your ride into work? Did you look around to check out some of the faces on the bus, on the subway, or in the car next to yours? Did you take time to daydream, even if just for a moment? Did you take time to plan, to pat yourself on the back for a job well done? Making time to enjoy the moment isn't being selfish—it makes one whole.

Time is borrowed; therefore, we should never get comfortable with it because it is not ours. We must learn to make it work for us by mastering it. When we say master it, we mean take control of time while we have it. Each second should be used to get us closer to our desired goals. If we fail to seize the moment, our goals and dreams will stagnate.

Fear and time are like oil and water—they do not mix. It is fear that prevents us from taking risks which can result in missing opportunity when it presents itself. Success happens in time, but first we must risk something. That something is usually a thing, person, or place that prevents us from applying the proper time needed to accomplish our aims.

Luck means being prepared when an opportunity presents itself. However, the unlucky time is still essential because we learn from that how to be more certain when opportunity presents itself, hence making time work for us. This enables you to seize the moment the second time around more fearlessly. Fear prevents success.

Nobody plans to fail in life. We fail to plan in life by not taking the time to strategize a way to better our lives. Time is how life is measured. Therefore, when we waste time we are wasting life. We must take control of our lives in order to make them better. The time to do so is now.

SOUL REVEALING QUESTIONS

- Describe how you have stepped out on faith.

- How do you look at your life?

- Do you pray?

- Do you have a spiritual relationship with God?

- Describe how your faith has been easily wavered or increased over time. Give details.

- Do you call on God only when there is a crisis, or do you have an ongoing relationship with God?

- When you're in the middle of a crisis are you able to surrender to God?

- Have you faced a health crisis and if so, how were you able to work through it?

- What gifts do you believe that God has given you?

- How do you plan to have your gifts work to help your fellow sisters?

- What would you like to bring closure to? What are you most grateful for?

Revelations Revealed:

Dream big, embrace your challenges; use the power of prayer and the spiritual message presented in your life as empowerment to better your relationship with God. Here is a quote from Marianne Williamson that we believe will help you get to your spiritual awakening:

"Our deepest fear is not that we are inadequate. Our deepest fear is that we are powerful beyond measure. We ask ourselves, 'Who am I to be brilliant, gorgeous, talented, and fabulous?' ACTUALLY, WHO ARE YOU NOT TO BE?"

When you get to the moment of realization that you are brilliant, gorgeous, talented, and absolutely and unequivocally fabulous, you are awake!

Your Revelations Revealed:

CHAPTER 7

Transformation of Spirit

If only a transformation was as easy as picking up this book or purchasing a DVD. It requires a commitment to change and is a prerequisite for African-American women in order to create peace in their lives. It is like peeling an onion—there are layers, the roughest being the outer layer, and when each layer is peeled back the essence of the onion emerges, bringing with it tears. You can't get to the true essence without the tears and that is the part worth using, the part we all want to get to. Khalil Gibran stated, "Your pain is the breaking of the shell that encloses your understanding. Even as the stone of the fruit must break, that its heart may stand in the sun, so must you know pain."

We went through a transition before the completion of this book. Although we were good at a lot of different things individually, nothing brought us greater joy than working with the women of *Souls of My Sisters*. Regardless of what we did, whether it was as individuals or as a team, somehow it would revert back to the empowerment of women.

At first we shrank back because the release of the first

book took so much out of us. We were on the road almost every weekend and did seminars and book signings for a number of years while maintaining pretty heady careers. We felt that it took time away from our lives, not recognizing it was expanding our horizons. Candace remembers having a conversation with a very good male friend who was also a reporter who recently was married and confided in him that she wanted to get married and have a baby and perhaps not pursue this dream. He was so harsh with his advice that it startled her. He said, "The husband and baby will come— don't even worry about it. Follow your dream or else you will grow to hate your life." Hate was such a strong word, but he had a point.

We never set out to make this an enterprise—our intention was to contribute to the healing of black women and in the process create stronger women within ourselves. Nothing was feeling right and we knew that if we took our individual talents and focused them on a common goal that we both enjoyed, it would reap significant benefits.

We made a SWOT analysis (a marketing measuring tool for business that gauges Strengths, Weaknesses, Obstacles, and Threats) for our business, and included our personal attributes in a diagram. We had a strong brand and in order to get that brand in the hands of more women, we needed to be truthful within ourselves. We focused on environment, physical health, and spiritual healing, also ridding our lives of toxic people and learning to set limits.

There were significant setbacks at the outset. Candace was

extremely sick with migraines and exhaustion that she was being monitored by an internist, neurologist, physical therapist and a nutritionist three times a week, there were major pressures with her job, and then her family suffered a major death. I became ill and had to have an operation and coincidentally my mother was diagnosed with stage 2 ovarian cancer and my children started being teenagers in every aspect of that word.

Candace's boyfriends started to act up and out. Friends became few and distant and some of this continued to happen just as we were about to swing our doors open for business. I was dealing with the contractor from below hell and taking care of my ailing parents. Things all seemed off balance, and we felt like what could happen next? This transformation felt like our lives had been turned inside out and we were being wrung out of every last bit of energy we had.

Your transformation is your own—it may be moving into a new home, having a child, getting married, losing a job, or deciding to leave a relationship. It is uncertain and uncharted territory. The basic truth is that growth requires pain and there are no quick fixes or shortcuts, but spiritual transformation is the first step toward healing ourselves.

We coined the word *rehabitants* to describe some of the celebrities who make headlines and constantly go in and out of rehabilitation centers and clinics. But are we also rehabitants who are going in and out of patterns and practices in our lives? Whether you are changing a life pattern or dealing with addiction, it requires a process steeped in truth, discipline, obedience, and faith. We must learn how to handle situations, not regretting the past, serene in the understanding that God has a greater purpose for our lives.

Finding out what our true purpose is requires work. More often than not our purpose is right in front of us, yet we spend most of our lives running from that responsibility. Once you slow down and recognize that this is your path in life and you begin your journey, you will start to understand your purpose. What is interesting is that most of us would never think of setting off on a road trip without a map, directions, and a telephone number for our final destination, just in case. But we live our lives without a plan, or even an addendum to one that is already in place. Now it's time to create a life plan that incorporates your mental, physical, and spiritual growth. The new life plan keeps you on course toward your goals and adds new passions picked up along the way. You also need to examine your commitment to make the necessary changes, and look at your life from another perspective. Are you willing to pay the ultimate price? Are you ready to put forth the effort and the discipline required? Can you sustain yourself through a transition? Is your desire strong enough to instill and implement the discipline needed to accomplish your objective? We hope so because you will need to make the ultimate life commitment to yourself.

Visualization

One of the most important things you can do for yourself is enjoy who you are. Your life will be constantly filled with challenges, tasks, joys, and opportunities that you had no idea were in the making. Close your eyes and visualize your experience, feel the emotions of all of the highs and lows in your life. Nothing else matters more than the relationship you have with God. Take a moment to look at the landscape of your life. In the book *The Secret*, Rhonda Byrne describes cutting out pictures and creating visualization boards, a physical reminder that can lead to a self-fulfilling prophecy that will give you a clear understanding of what you want.

Creating a SWOT Analysis

A SWOT analysis is usually performed by a diverse group of individuals in an organization with an end goal in mind. This analysis can also be a valuable tool in assessing your own personal strengths, weaknesses, opportunities, and threats. It provides a powerful insight into the potential and critical issues affecting your life. Your end goals should be self-improvement and healing.

Make a list of your strengths, which are the attributes that you like and appreciate about yourself. Showcase your advantages and your capabilities. Make a list of your weaknesses—what are the patterns and practices that you wish to change? Does your reputation precede you? What are you famous for? Explore the opportunities available to you. Examine some of the barriers that you would consider to be your weaknesses. Threats are internal or external issues that could affect you. Make a list of what you believe would be barriers to the execution of your plan. Outside threats can result from toxic people who are ready and willing to challenge you and attempt to plant the seeds of doubt. They will say things like, "It will never happen," or, "Why waste your time?"

SWOT ANALYSIS

Strengths	Weaknesses
Opportunities	Threats

Once you have come up with your strengths, weaknesses, opportunities, and threats, you will need to examine everything that is USED. Here are questions you need to answer:

How can I Use each strength?
How can you better use your strengths to accomplish your goals? Did you realize you had more strengths than you originally thought?

How can I Stop each weakness?
How can you stop your bad habits dead in their tracks? How can you improve upon your weaknesses until they are no longer weaknesses?

How can I **Exploit** each opportunity?
How can you better recognize opportunities in your life?
How can you learn to seize the moment when opportunities present themselves?

How can I **Defend** against each threat?
How can you build up your spiritual armor to defend against any external threat? How can you become ready for mental, spiritual, or physical attack?

Every Step Counts

As you take action in your plan each day, even the smallest steps lead to big changes. Everything in life requires work and you owe it to yourself to work hard, stand firm, and know that all things are possible through God. You deserve a greater life, one that is fulfilling and aligned with what inspires and excites you. The only things separating you from your objective are action, time, and patience.

Setbacks are inevitable—prepare yourself for them and have a contingency plan in place. As you progress with your plan, tweak it along the way, record what happens, and most of all, just keep going.

Reward Yourself for Progress

Celebrate with each milestone or benchmark. As you become more connected with and committed to a transformation, all of the hard work will yield amazing rewards. Take a few days off; treat yourself to something special because you deserve it.

Transformation brings with it rich rewards but before you reap these benefits you will be besieged with chaos, and you will feel as if you are in your own personal hell. You start to question things and may become temporarily paralyzed due to fear. Your natural instinct will say run as fast as you can, back to a comfortable space, or just crawl under your covers. Hiding would never work because once a shift in your thinking happens it becomes increasingly harder to ignore it. What we noticed in our own personal experience is that with each and every task or challenge, we came out on the other side stronger as individuals and feeling a tremendous amount of gratitude for the process.

Once you have come to the realization that you have tipped the scales in your spiritual favor, you begin to sense a renewing of your mind. People who have known you for years will ask you what you have done to yourself. Transformation of spirit is that breakthrough point where you can't help but smile—like you know something everyone else doesn't. It is the beginning of your true revelation. It is that realization point when all things seem new, as if you are looking at them for the first time.

SOUL REVEALING QUESTIONS

- What don't you like about yourself and your life?

- What would you like to change?

- What do you believe are your greatest strengths?

- Are you open to a life change at this time? And how hard will change be for you?

- If you are considering a life change, what would be your time frame? Are your intentions to begin right now? Within three to six months?

- What would be the two top life goals that you would like to pursue?

- What could be your potential roadblocks?

- What are the biggest concerns that could threaten your plan?

- Who do you know who can inspire you?

- What will be the financial cost of attaining your goals?

- Will you need to seek help? What would be the best possible way to do that?

Revelations Revealed:

"Personal transformation can and does have global effects. As we go, so goes the world, for the world is us. The revolution that will save the world is ultimately a personal one."—Marianne Williamson.

Your Revelations Revealed:

CHAPTER 8

Reevaluating the Role of Money in Your Life

Each one of us basically has the same desires—to be happy, healthy, and prosperous. We ask ourselves why it is that prosperity has eluded some not others. Some may ask, how come I have everything, and yet I am still not happy? We have met so many women, some of them extremely rich and powerful, and although they enjoy their lifestyles, they are usually unhappy. Many of them, and perhaps even you, too, thought that money or marrying the right husband would bring them happiness. Money alone cannot make you happy. It can only enhance and enrich a life filled with balance, self-worth, love, respect, honor, and passion for your purpose.

John H. Johnson, founder of Johnson Publishing, is now deceased. In *Succeeding Against the Odds,* he wrote that when his company exceeded $100 million he was told by a bank officer that he needed to engage a large white accounting firm and not the black one he had used since he opened the doors to his business. "That is when I realized that the power and witchery of money is, with the possible exception of sex, the most fascinating subject in the world. Like sex, money inhabits a realm that transcends machines and numbers. Money can be counted, measured, weighed, but it can't be predicted. Always and everywhere it overshadows the experience, giving you more or less of what you expected. There is no balance when it comes to money. You either have too much or too little. When you don't have it, you work like the devil to get it. And when you have it, you work like the devil to keep it."

Everyone, and we mean everyone, at some point in their life has some type of money issues. The habits that you form in your life dictate whether you run like the devil, patiently building your wealth, horde your earnings because you've come from lean means, or serve your wealth on a cold dish called revenge, flaunting your success.

Time magazine's recent cover article read, "Faith and Prosperity: Does God Want You to Be Rich?" This disputes the teachings of various preachers but tells the story of how many parishioners were inspired by their preachers' insistence that one of God's top priorities is to shower blessings on Christians in this lifetime. By corollary assumption, one of the worst things a person can do is to expect anything less— regardless of your economic status or circumstance, it is the soulful choice as to how you choose to live your life which decides your destination. Your money habits were instilled in you before you were even aware of them.

Some of us are great planners—we start putting together our retirement portfolios and save for our children's college funds before they are conceived. But most of us are not as diligent and it is the "in between" that we are really not prepared for. In a twinkle of an eye the unpredictability of life can change the landscape. It comes in all forms, including caring for an ailing parent or parents, the illness of a partner, child, or yourself, the house that never sold, or unexpected layoffs. You find yourself in a financial crisis and somewhere in all of this you ask yourself how you are supposed to enjoy your life with so much pressure?

Gwendolynn Quinn's Story

"Like most people, I love having and spending money. It's taken me a long time to respect money and get my spending habits under control. Quite frankly, I'm not totally there yet, but I am much better. I opened the doors to my company, GQ Media & Public Relations, in 2002. Prior to that I held several positions at various record labels and entertainment companies, including Capitol Records, Arista, Island, Mercury/PolyGram Records, Flavor Unit Entertainment, ASCAP, ABC-TV, and others. In my last corporate position as Vice President of Urban Publicity at Capitol Records, I was making a salary of $200,000, not including annual bonuses and fringes. Therefore, when I lost my job a few weeks after 9/11, I knew that my prospects for finding another position with that salary and title were going to be limited. I had just exited an industry during the end of its golden era.

"That was during the time when there was also a major shift in the music industry; although I was still under contract and was able to maintain my lifestyle for a while, I knew that my only viable option was to start my own company. I did not want to have my own business and I resented having to start it under these circumstances. I always had an entrepreneurial spirit, but starting a business was way too much work. I was just fine collecting a big paycheck. I have now been in business for nearly six years and during the first five, I went back and forth, contemplating finding a job, thinking being an entrepreneur was way too hard and very exhausting. I complained constantly.

"I didn't start my business the way most people do, with a business plan, a loan, a bookkeeper, a client list, etc. I had to start my business by default. There have been many peaks and valleys. Although I've managed to do a fairly good job at publicizing and promoting my firm and building a diverse client roster, I was not keeping my financial records in order or paying quarterly taxes. My company looked great to others, but some of my business matters were a big mess. In fact, I was several years behind on filing my taxes.

"I just recently got caught up, putting my financial records in order. At various points during my company's history, the revenues were up and down. There were times when I missed payroll for long periods; there were many times that I couldn't pay my vendors and several times when I was in default on my mortgage and nearly foreclosure bound. But each and every time, God has always been there to save me. And although things are not where they should be and I am constantly struggling to keep the doors of my company open, I have a clearer vision of the importance of building and keeping great credit, saving, and maintaining accurate and up-to-date financial records, as well as creating and developing multiple revenue streams. I love the freedom that comes with having my own business and I have accepted that this is the path that God has me on for now.

"There are many things that I am called to do. I know that I want to travel the world over and work with underprivileged children in various countries; I want to adopt as many kids as

I can afford. I now realize that having money and establishing wealth has a new meaning for me. Through God's will, I am determined to live out His purpose for my life—I am determined to achieve financial success in order to access those goals and have the things in life that are really important. Money does not have to be the ruler of all evil."

The Reverend Chestina Archibald, longtime chaplain at Fisk University, encourages us to seek prosperity as a way of reaping the abundance that God has planned for us. She quotes 3 John 2: "Beloved, I wish above all things that thou mayest prosper and be in health, even as thy soul prospereth." From His verses, we can emphatically know that God wants us to be in good health and enjoy prosperity. In fact, these days good finances are synonymous with better health and living conditions for our families and more opportunities to fulfill our responsibilities as servants and stewards of God's word. According to Reverend Archibald, it is not just a divine right to be prosperous—it is God's expectation that we use the best of the resources that He put before us. If we deny what God has intended for us, then we are also denying our rightful power to do God's will.

We equate riches with "fool's gold," and there is many a scripture where a person has fallen because of wanton ways and too much focus on worldly goods. Certainly, nowhere in the Bible do the words *lottery* or *bling* come into play. Yet the Bible is clear about how children should be cared for and our responsibility to our parents, let alone tithing. The idea that money corrupts is a concept that keeps us feeling noble in our poverty. The only kind of poverty that is noble is the type that you have eagerly chosen as a sacrifice to God. Chosen poverty means you have abstained from all worldly goods to focus your gifts on a divine purpose. Yet, involuntary poverty is no nobler than ignorance of your true purpose. If the power of money is used for corruption, then what could we accomplish if the power of money were in our hands and used for a more divine purpose?

But many of us are not struggling with wealth; we are struggling to survive. Many of us are just getting by. Pastors today are encouraging us to think beyond today and plan for tomorrow. The Reverend Dr. Michael Moore, pastor of Faith Chapel Christian Center and author of *Rich Is NOT A Bad Word,* asks; "Are you tired of living from paycheck to paycheck? Do you desire wealth and riches to be in your house for you and for others?" Then, he encourages us to "take hold of the truths of the scriptures that prove to us that God wants us to be prosperous." According to Dr. Moore, being rich and being a believer is very important, and there are spiritual laws that govern our marriages, health, faith, and even our finances.

Nowhere in the Bible does the word *lottery* appear. There is no synonym for *bling.*

How do your finances bring you closer to being the instrument that God would have you be in this world?

What might you gain by having your finances guided by the strength of the Spirit and the Will of God for you and your family to prosper?

Understanding how money works and how it can best serve you is critical for women. More people are in debt than ever before. Whether you are married, single, or divorced, you need to be prepared financially. Like women of the past, you no longer can depend on a man to take care of your financial needs.

If you are single, the tables have turned—men are also looking at your economic viability. Some men are willing to scam you, hoping to take advantage of your romantic weakness. The media perpetrates the get-rich-or-die-trying lifestyle. We have been sold on a life not worth living unless it is filled with excess. It has gone beyond the manic pace of keeping up with the Joneses.

Still other men are just as frustrated as you that it is almost impossible in some cities to raise a family on just one salary. Men recognize pretty quickly how burdensome it can be and are in search of a helpmate to create a level of comfort and stability.

On the other hand it becomes tricky because some men have fragile egos and can become irritated if they find out you make more than they do; others will be just fine with it. The key is finding someone who has his self-esteem intact.

Separating Fear From Finances

There is a Russian proverb that states, "When money speaks, the truth keeps silent." What keeps us silent is that we are afraid to ask questions and seek more information because there is a kind of shame associated with a lack of knowledge about money. We are also fearful of making a mistake so we end up repeating the same mistakes again and again. Candace went to a large firm to get financial advice and drive. The counselor was glowing about his client who socked away over $100,000 on a nurse's salary never going anywhere, just work and home for the last 20 years. Now that she put her daughter through college she was ready to invest. When he saw that Candace's investments were nowhere near that he grimaced. She got up and never went back. Women don't want to be slaves to money, just going to work and straight home, never taking a financial risk or enjoying their ability to save and still experience life. Women don't want to be judged, especially single women who face financially ignorant people each and every day when they go to purchase a home, car, or other big-ticket item.

What have you done with the money that has passed through your hands? Did you invest? Did you give some to charity? Sock some away for a rainy day? Used it to build memories for yourself and your family? Did you invest in your children's education? Did you have the wedding of your dreams? Did you see faraway places? Did you invest in you? Or do you have every designer shoe, dress, and handbag overflowing your closet?

In Souls of My Sisters *we talk about reviewing how and what you spend your money on:*

- Commit to paying off your debt.

- Build an emergency savings and have it deducted directly from your paycheck.

- Think about ways in which to invest your money wisely in items that will appreciate.

It is never too late to reevaluate your finances and start thinking smart about money. We use money or credit as an emotional fix that can't be repaired.

SOUL REVEALING QUESTIONS

- What is your belief about money?

- How did your family handle money?

- What are your money goals?

- How much stress does money cause in your life?

- Do you live beyond your means?

- Do you impulse-buy or do you evaluate your desires versus your needs?

- What do you do with money? Do you tend to save, spend, or invest?

- When was the last time you checked your credit? What is your score?

- How much money do you spend on personal care—hair, nails, etc.?

- Do you have outstanding debts?

- How much money do you need to feel comfortable?

- What are your retirement plans?

- How would you handle an unexpected life change, job loss, etc.?

- Are you willing to provide financial support to your partner?

- How do you feel about being supported by a partner?

- What is the best money advice that works for you?

Revelations Revealed:

"Your money or your life." We know *what to do when a burglar makes this demand of us, but not when God does.*—Mignon McLaughlin, *The Second Neurotic's Notebook,* 1966

Your Revelations Revealed:

CHAPTER 9

Collective Healing

When you experience your personal revelation it is a miraculous feeling to have the answers to the questions that have been holding you back, but the truth of the revelation isn't just for you to keep to yourself. A revelation wouldn't be a true revelation unless you shared its power with someone else. As we saw with *Souls of My Sisters,* the testimonies the women were sharing were not just for individuals. They were blessed with their revelations so that they could share them and start a collective healing for women of color. It is our responsibility and the true meaning and purpose of our revelations.

Collective healing is what we strive for in the pages of this book. The women were brave enough to share their stories and begin to work on the issues and be supportive of one another without judgment or recourse. The collective healing will help build a deeper meaning in life for ourselves and for all those around us.

UCLA published a study in 2004 that proves that women interacting with other women can actually counteract the kind of stomach-quivering stress most of us experience on a daily basis.

The discovery that women respond to stress differently than men was made in a classic "aha" moment shared by two women scientists who were talking one day in a lab at UCLA. A popular joke stated that when the women who worked in the lab were stressed, they came in, cleaned the lab, had coffee, and bonded, says Dr. Cousino Klein now an Assistant Professor of Biobehavioural Health at Penn State University and one of the study's authors. When the men were stressed, they holed up somewhere on their own. Study after study has found that social ties reduce our risk of disease by lowering blood pressure, heart rate, and cholesterol. "There's no doubt," says Dr. Klein, "that friends are helping us live longer."

When people are depressed they tend to become introverts and go into isolation. The reason for this, I believe, is because they feel that no one else can relate to what they are going through. It is not until they acknowledge that they are not alone in their distress that they begin to recover from their depression. It helps when they find a person who has recovered from that state which plagues them. Then they have hope of emulating that person, hence the beginning of their healing process.

We all look for answers to our problems, finding the best solutions from those who have experience with our current situations. Not only do they help to solve our problems, but they give us the courage to face them. They will not criticize or judge harshly because they can relate and understand. This is the reason places like Alcoholics Anonymous are beneficial. People go through a collective healing process along with others who share their problem.

However, it does not always take somebody who has been through the same exact experience to reach out and help us. It can be someone who overcame a completely different problem. Just by revealing the techniques they used, they can help us.

It's the "each one teach one" philosophy. When someone helps us find the answers to our problems, the best way to return the favor is by helping another. It's mutual trust and respect that establishes the bond.

But What Happens When That Trust and Respect Is Breached?

A colleague shared her recent experience of a rift between two black women, both working at a major university. A clerical staff member—we'll call her Ann—and a professor—we'll call her Jackie—were working on a project together when they came to an impasse. Both felt passionate about and engaged in the project, but Ann felt bullied and belittled by Jackie. Ann felt that the professor offered suggestions and was quick to move ahead without integrating Ann's comments into the project. When Jackie tells the story, she says she felt disrespected and questioned by Ann because of all the back and forth in her approach. In the end they were not able to finish the project that they both felt so passionately about. The problem wasn't Ann's insistence that she be heard, or even Jackie's approach. The issue was bigger than that—it was trust and respect. Jackie felt that if Ann were talking to a white professor, her tone and demeanor would have been different. Ann agrees, but she came at it from a different angle. Ann didn't treat Jackie differently because she didn't respect her but because she felt comfortable enough to be herself.

We must learn to trust and respect one another in our professional lives and find ways to address the most important issues so we can move on. The example that we offered took place on a college campus, but we could have been describing a local church, a parent-teacher organization, or a civic group. In any of these organizations, you can see some of the same problems occurring. We can be cool and cordial with one another but when it comes down to it, some of us may be holding our sisters to a different standard than we hold other people to. We have to work on our issues of trust and respect. It is imperative for our collective network of sisters to be honest with each other, not just about our feelings but about our well-thought-out strategies for change.

Asking for Help

In order to get help, we must first acknowledge the fact that we are sometimes helpless. As Mary J. Blige put it, "We have been 'too strong for too long.' " Maybe that strength is also a weakness if it keeps us from risking a position of vulnerability and being able to simply say, "I need help." What do we lose by asking for help? We lose the right to say, "I did it myself." We also lose the opportunity to be martyrs and queens of suffering and sacrifice. We lose that feeling of being independent to the point that we don't have to rely on anyone else or worry about being let down. Yet, what would happen if we were to go to our collective healing space and call in our backup? We would gain a network of support to help us find a straighter path to our goals. We'd help to form a closer bond among women looking to bring change to their lives and make a difference in this world. We'd gain the opportunity to let go of the lie that it is possible to do it "by our damn selves." By learning to say "I need help," we give others permission to do the same. Ask for help more often and notice how many people are able to lend a hand and able to share not only their successes but also their own vulnerabilities with you in the future. When we share our shortcomings we let others borrow our mistakes so they don't have to go out and step in those same traps. As a reciprocal action, we each can benefit from that same kind of give and take. Just think how much more successful your next stage of life can be by multiplying each of the lessons learned by the number of sisters in your network. That's the power of our collective healing.

Be intentional about building your healing network. Find other women with similar desires by doing more than just inviting them to your latest pity party. Instead, look toward people you admire and emulate the way they make things go well in their lives. Don't focus on the things they have but on the way they have created success in their lives. Then pay them the ultimate compliment and ask them how they do it and see if they will share their secrets. We have found that women are very willing to share their gifts with others.

Whether it is a really organized kitchen or a great plan for getting three kids up and out the door in the morning, we can find some of our best ideas just from asking women about their successful strategies. These strategies are not only good for helpful home hints—we can learn a lot from women that we admire about character, tenacity and the will that it takes to succeed. Create a network and encourage one another by focusing on career, financial, and personal goals. Not sure how to land a job in a new field or start an investment club? Give each other assignments to find out information and share it with the group. As Cheryl Broussard, author of *Sister CEO*, tells us, we should "network with other successful black women and ask them how they overcame their insecurities. Challenges are lessons that we must learn. When we understand this, then we can begin to move forward."

Creating your collective healing network:

1. Identify women you would enjoy spending more time with, knowing you could benefit from their advice.

2. Set a theme for your interactions—a family network, finance group, or a book club. Having focus for your group doesn't minimize the fun, it gives your network urgency and purpose.

3. Set personal goals and share them with your network. Goal-setting is a good way to insure that you stay on task and move toward the changes you wish to see in your life.

4. Celebrate your success with milestones. Don't just celebrate birthdays, marriages, and new houses. How about a get-together to celebrate the fact that one of the women in your network has gotten a new job?

5. Don't forget to reflect. Whether a transition is positive or negative, there is a lesson that the group can sort through. Take the time to notice the signs that God is helping you through the changes that occur in your life. Be open to feedback from these women who know you best and care about you. Their praise and constructive guidance will help you to see your path even more clearly.

PLATEAU OF LIFE

Doing things out of habit? Stuck in a rut? Get in the habit of being enthusiastic and positive. Our feelings are infectious. What do you want people to say they caught from you? A cold, the flu? Or joy, a smile, and a positive attitude? It is your choice. When we feel good about ourselves and we see good in the world around us, then that means that every day we are given God testimony and praise for what He has done for us and through us.

How do we break those old habits and sail past the plateau of life where we feel we have gotten just enough joy, just enough pay in our current job, or just enough of a good standard of living for our family? We break past "just enough" by moving forward with our desires to manage what we can control in our lives.

What Do We Control?

Believe it or not, there is much less in our control than we actually imagine. By focusing on those things that we can control, we actually may feel more powerful in times of uncertainty. So, what are the things that are actually in our control? What we *control* is weighed against what's in our *influence* and what is our *concern*.

Your area of concern is global issues that impact the world but may not affect your day-to-day life, things going on with people you care about. The homeless problem, the high cost of living, and education across the country are all things that we might be concerned with but we don't have control over.

Influence is another story. We can influence our child's behavior by making sure he gets enough rest, has a good breakfast, and fully understands the consequences of acting out in class. We can't pick our bosses but we can influence their attitude toward us by playing up our strengths. We can influence someone's feelings for us by giving them the space they need, listening when they talk, and focusing on pleasing them instead of ourselves. Our area of influence includes things that we can do something about to impact the people or systems around us. When we go to work and keep notes on our performance and it results in a better evaluation over time, that's exerting our influence.

So, what is in our CONTROL? Control has to do with the actual thoughts, feelings, and beliefs we have and the expression of those feelings.

SOUL REVEALING QUESTIONS

● Are your family and friends supportive of your goals? Do they encourage you? Or do they put down your efforts?

● Who are some of the people you know who have obtained similar goals? How did they do it?

● How do you handle setbacks? Do you access the reasons behind the setback and address those issues?

Revelations Revealed:

I, like my sisters, am a vessel for God's wisdom and love. I will share the information and healing I have found with my sisters to create a momentous movement of love and sisterhood. I know that everything I have received will grow if I share it amongst my sisters.

Your Revelations Revealed:

CHAPTER 10

Victory Revealed

Once you have done the work, how do you maintain your spirit and continue to create new revelations on your life's journey? Like someone who has lost weight, maintenance is the key. The process will always work but you must be diligent and true to the change that occurs due to your revelation. The process is not a one-time thing but an all-the-time thing, and the victory is in the continuity of spirit.

Imagine that the world is your oyster and that abundance and prosperity are available to you. How would you behave at work? What would that feeling do for your interactions at church or at home? Feelings of scarcity reinforce the baseless fear that God only rationed out a limited amount of love, grace, and good luck to the world. By feeling like the damned instead of the blessed, we lose the opportunity to keep the door open to abundance and joy. Claim victory by using words each day that bring you closer to the life you expect to have. Don't doubt that God can provide that life for you. Imagine good things and then act as if those good things are going to happen. This is not easily done because we have

155

spent more time being realistic in our past—realistic, meaning depressive, negative, and doubtful. But what if realistic could mean exciting, positive, and certain! The only difference between the first definition of realistic and the second is perspective.

Frankia Granberry, a doctoral student at the University of Chicago, and Dr. Jarralynne Agee did research on the coping skills of African-American residents of New Orleans after the Katrina devastation. They went into their research project expecting to find ways that people coped, survived and managed after the storm. However, shortly after arriving in New Orleans they saw that they had to change their frame of reference to match the attitude of these heroic people. When they asked how they survived after the storm, people answered in a totally different way than expected.

"Survive?" they said. "I am not a survivor—my cousin Joe, he was a survivor. I was stranded for two days in my attic. He was stranded for four days with no food, and he barely made it. He's a survivor, honey. I am BLESSED."

Frankia, the doctoral student, was quick to make modifications. She went out to New Orleans prepared to ask her second question, how are you coping after the storm? Again, the answers debunked all expectations.

"Coping?" they said. "Coping with what? Sure, I am not happy about the fact that my parents live in Texas and my children are in Mississippi and I had to come back here. But if I wallow in pity, then I am disrespecting hundreds of people who are separated from their families by a long bus trip. Some of their family is just gone." They went on to say, "I am not coping, honey. Coping can only get you from day to day. I am living, because that's what God let me stay on this earth for, so I'd best get to living."

Frankia consulted with Dr. Linda James Myers, a prominent Afrocentric psychologist from Ohio State University, who encouraged her to abandon a rigid set of academic questions and ask one simple question: "How do you make sense of what has happened here?" The question, simple on its surface, acknowledges the storm and the terrible damage it caused and the lives that it took. But it does something else—it allows the responder to share their "worldview" and the way they see their current situation. A worldview, according to Dr. Myers, is a way of looking at the world; it is a philosophical or cultural lens that colors the way you interpret things, how you make decisions, and how you find meaning in the information handed to you.

When asked the worldview question, "How do you make sense of what has happened here?," the responders did not talk about coping, managing, and surviving as the research team originally thought they would. Instead the New Orleans residents discussed something altogether different.

Instead of feeling picked on and targeted by God's wrath, they told the researchers the following:

"I felt God washed away my sins."

"The flooding water was a rebirth for me and for our city."

Instead of trying to find ways to manage the horrible events that had happened to them, they said:

"I don't try to question why the storm happened. I don't even try to damn the storm. But I do try to make sense of my purpose and why God chose me to stay. I can't dwell in the past; I have to find meaning for my future."

Finally, when the researchers wanted to know the secret of their coping strategies, they simply sat back and listened to what the people of the city had to say. Mayor Ray Nagin told the research team:

"I can't speak for everybody else on how they cope. But for me, I get in the Word every day and try to become one with the Lord."

What can we learn from these believers? We can learn that although we may experience adversity, we still have a choice as to how we interpret the events of our lives. No matter how harsh or how tragic, it is our frame of reference that determines our ability to weather the storm. We are kindred spirits with the people of New Orleans, and some of you reading the words in this book are those very same people. So therefore, we need to know that we are made of the very stuff that creates not only survivors but people who have chosen to live!

On a personal note for us, as the Katrina tragedy hit we watched it from our New York television stations and immediately mobilized to provide support and aid. Since that time we have had innumerable conversations with women who have made a plan to make a way out of no way. Changing your frame of reference is the first step in choosing to live. Finding the right resources, networks, and information is the next step that helps turn positive thoughts into positive action. Whether it is Katrina survivors, families of the World Trade Center tragedy, or individuals suffering alone, people are learning that they are stronger than they thought. The courage and wisdom and strength of the people of New Orleans provide valuable lessons for all of us.

Maintaining Our Victory

We know that it's hard for many of us to think in this transformative way so we are providing some ideas to help you reframe your thinking. What we can learn from people who show faith and courage after a storm is that they find a new way to look at things. In fact, they have found ways to turn adversity into advantage. How can that be, you ask? How can the people who survived the storm be better off than those who were warm and dry in their homes? Because they have had a life-altering shift in thinking.

They will never look at things the same as they did. Things we take for granted have new and expanded meaning for them. Joy is relative and they recognize one's attitude as a choice. Tom Delvin, a West Coast career counselor, helped Katrina college students who had made it all the way to colleges like Stanford, UC Berkeley, and Fresno State to realize that their adversity was also an advantage.

Tom encouraged each of the displaced Katrina college students to redo their resumes or graduate school applications to reflect what we call an "adversity advantage." He told them, "When you found a college that would take you in and drove 2000 miles across country, that showed your TENACITY."

He continued, "When you called every school and got your transcript sent out by posting it on Facebook and having friends print it out and take it to the registrar . . . that showed your *facilitation of networking and resourcefulness.*"

He instructed them to reframe their thinking. Instead of saying, "I am a Katrina refugee who had a rough junior year," tell them, "my experiences that I didn't choose but couldn't have learned in any classroom or corporation make me a more empathetic, driven, and resourceful asset to your graduate program or business."

The Principles of the Adversity Advantage

Currently there are fewer than fifty psychologists in the entire city of New Orleans, so the city is finding a way to heal itself using their collective spirit of survival. Working with Dr. Jarralynne Agee, who was the lead researcher of the post-Katrina trip, we have outlined the lessons that each of us can take away from the transformation that happened to the people of New Orleans.

Great leaders not only fail, they learn to fail. They take the lessons learned from their shortcomings and turn them into foundations for success.

Change your mind and change your life.

When we feel that God has given us nothing else, know that He has always given us the power to choose how we respond and the option to seek help.

Focusing on despair doesn't solve the problem, it expands it.

Conversely, focusing on action that can lead you away from problems and despair doesn't expand the issue, it counteracts it.

Find a network that you love and trust, then find a way to be the biggest contributor in your group and make sure that when you rise, they rise, too. They will return the favor.

How do you turn your own adversity into advantage?

By figuring out what you learned and gained from your unique experience. Think of what characteristics and traits you now possess that make you a better person, friend, or employee. Your past limitations should not be a hindrance to your future aspiration. Your circumstances need to be the backdrop for your rise from the ashes or the flood waters.

What can you create if you acted like the New Orleans residents and behaved as if every day is a gift and that your life was something special with a divine purpose?

Exercise: "At least" and "As if"

In order to retrieve you from life support we have to change our words. Let's take your "at least" statements and shift the perspective toward something that we can actually use. Think of your "at least" statements as anchors on your ship of life. Now our goal is to change our perspective enough to pull up those anchors and turn on the propeller to move us forward. At first you might feel totally stuck, but if you really think about it, those "at least" statements show us where there is a bright light in some of the dark areas in life. Let's build on what's right by analyzing our self-talk.

1. The Good Stuff. Look at your "at least" statements and go back and circle those things that you are most proud of. You might have some statements that you aren't really proud of and we aren't focusing on those right now. We are looking for your success stories. Find them, circle them or highlight them, but make sure that whenever you look at it you see the good.

2. Rephrasing. Take the items you have circled and find a way to turn them into completely positive statements. No qualifier. For example, "At least, I have a new boss" now becomes, "I have a new boss and a new beginning at my worksite." Some of the statements may need re-wording to find the positives.
    For example, "At least he stopped hitting me" could become, "I have stopped accepting the pain of being hurt by him."

3. Make your new statements. Your new "as if" statements should focus on what you want out of life—the "as if" is the connector between what is real and what you expect, not just what you will accept.

For example, "I will stop accepting the pain of being hurt by him AS IF my daughter's happiness depended on it." Or, "I will start to act more engaged at work AS IF my new boss is interested in building a great work space." These new statements not only focus on what you want, they focus on what you will do. And what's more, these statements help you to anticipate a positive outcome.

Change Maintenance

Sustainable change is important if we are interested in seeing real transformation. The way to stay on the course toward sustainable change is to focus on the outcomes you seek. If you are not sure if your behaviors are working for you, look at the outcomes created as a result of your regular interactions with people from day to day. An exercise that could help you focus is to chart what type of impact your feelings have on the world around you. Your interactions can manifest through expressed feelings, behaviors, and thoughts. However, these are simply types of behavior. We don't know what someone is thinking or feeling until they say or do something about it. So to create new outcomes in our lives we must manage our behavior successfully.

Remarkable Steps

Dr. Jarralynne Agee believes, "Create a series of remarkable steps that insure you stay focused on the dream and not stuck in your current situation. The first remarkable step is to stay connected and tuned in to people who think in the ideal. Notice how many of them are experiencing a style of life that is more in tune with what you expect for yourself. They may be happier and richer, but don't focus on what they have and what you don't have. Instead, focus on the energy that they used to move toward their ideal and then borrow some of that energy for you. Most people living their dream are willing to share their energy. Another remarkable step is to consistently focus on the ideal."

Dr. Agee continues, "Consider your current situation temporary. People who stay focused overestimate the negative impact of setbacks on their current situation. Those who tend to focus on the ideal see setbacks as road bumps, not roadblocks on their path. If you see your current situation as transient, you will put in motion a timeline for making better decisions in your life. The timeline is an essential step in moving toward your ideal. If you don't have a timeline for yourself, then someone else will provide one for you—and you don't want that. In fact, it's dangerous to let someone else determine your timeline because it's often in their best interest to convince you to stay where you are. In some ways your acceptance of a less than ideal position might suit their purpose just fine."

There is a part of prayer that says, "Help me to accept the things I cannot change." But it is also possible to use this as an excuse not to change. Of course, you cannot change someone else's actions, thoughts, ideals, opinions. You can influence them, but it is up to the person to change them. You also cannot change events of nature, accident, or disaster. What you can change is yourself, and to realize that your actions, deeds, and success is up to you is using forward, not fatalistic, thinking.

Dr. Agee continues, "Another step in getting unstuck is to create a plan of realistic action." It may not be possible for you to put down this book and then proceed to immediately leave your situation. Even if you can't jump all the way out of it now, how about tomorrow? And the next day. Learn the steps you can take each day to help get you into the next job, relationship, or opportunity. Do the work that it takes in increments so it won't feel like such an unimaginable leap. Finally, assess your current situation and begin to address what your real barriers are. These could concern education, health, or finances, but they are probably workable by using the proactive steps. Align yourself with inspirational people, plan the steps it takes to get there, and more than anything, focus on the ideal. Soon you will find yourself basking in the light of your new, more positive reality.

VICTORY BRAINSTORM

Step #1—Brainstorm "What's Not Working." Think of all of the issues keeping you from making systematic and dramatic change in your life. Write all of these down on a sheet of paper. If it's a person, name them. If it's an issue, describe it.

Step #2—Brainstorm "What Works Well." Jot down all the supportive things that you have going for you that help you move toward change. These can be both big and little things. They can be personal and impersonal. If you care about it, if it affects you, write it down.

Step #3—Take your "What's NOT Working" list and organize your statements using the descriptions of what is in your Concern, your Influence, or your Control.

Step #4—Take your "What Works Well" list and organize your statements using the descriptions of what is in your Concern, your Influence, or your Control.

Reflection on Your Life Change

What is in your area of concern? Are there things there that don't belong to you? Maybe they belong to someone else in your life, or maybe you can pray over them and give them to God. Focusing on things that are in your concern distract you from the work you could and should be doing. What do you have in your area of influence that helps you plan better for how you need to use your energy? Instead of going head-to-head with a bad boss or an ex-husband, how about focusing on the areas where you do have influence to help level the playing field and perhaps build a better relationship and outcome for yourself. Finally, what is in your control? If your "control" list is very small, it means you are very focused on what you could be doing or it might mean that there is more that you could be doing but don't know where to start. Engage the women in your network to help you look at the things you can control and help you to understand and use the power you have right now. If you had lots of information in your control area, that could mean that you are taking on a lot of the responsibility that might be shared with other people in your network. By taking on too much, we run the risk of not being able to have the impact we wish to have over time. You can draw your area of change out like large circles and help yourself get focused on what you do control.

My Area of Life Change

Concern:

Things I care about but can't influence.

(These may be world events, other people's feelings, and things from the past.)

Influence:

Things I can have an impact on through other people and organizations.

(These may be people's feelings about you, local events, and information sharing to help people make informed decisions.)

"Opinion is a fleeting thing, but truth outlasts the sun."
—Emily Dickinson

Spiritually Uplifting Books

Black Women's Lives: Stories of Pain and Power by Kristal Brent Zook. Nation Books, 2006

Childbirth Without Fear: The Principles of Natural Childbirth by Michel Odent, Grantly Dick-Read. Printer & Martin Publishers, 2005

Cinematherapy for the Soul: The Girl's Guide to Finding Inspiration One Movie at a Time by Nancy Peske, Beverly West. Bantam Doubleday Dell Publishing Group, 2004

Contesting the Terrain of the Ivory Tower: Spiritual Leadership of African-American Women in the Academy by Rochelle Garner. Taylor & Francis Books, 2004

Gems for the Journey by Vikki Johnson. Harlequin Books, 2005

His Rules: God's Practical Road Map for Becoming and Attracting Mr. or Mrs. Right by Christopher Burge and Pamela Toussaint. WaterBrook Press, 2005

Hugs for Women On the Go: Stories, Sayings, and Scriptures to Encourage and Inspire by Stephanie Howard, Leann Weiss. Simon & Schuster Adult Publishing Group, 2002

I Call You Friend: Four Women's Stories of Race, Faith, and Friendship by Pamela Toussaint, Jo Kadlecek. Broadman & Holman Publishers, 1999

I'm Too Blessed to Be Depressed by Joanna Campbell Slan. EFG, Inc., 2001

Leaning on Prayer: A Woman's Journey to Paradise and Back by Jerri A. Harwell. Spring Creek Book Company, 2004

Letter From the Holy Ground: Seeing God Where You Are by Loretta Ross-Gotta. Rowman & Littlefield Publishers, Inc., 2004

Love Made Visible by Paul Brenner, Susan Wingate. Council Oak Books, 2005

Mama's Little Baby: The Black Woman's Guide to Pregnancy, Childbirth, and Baby's First Year by Dennis Brown and Pamela Toussaint. Plume, 1998

Miracles of Motherhood: Prayers and Poems for A New Mother by June Cotner. Hachette Book Group USA, 2007

More Joy for the Journey: A Woman's Book of Joyful Promises by Terri Gibbs (editor), J. Countryman. Thomas Nelson, Inc., 2007

One Year Book of Devotions to Women by Jill Briscoe. Tyndale House, Inc., 2002

Prayers That Avail Much for Mothers: James 5:16, by Germaine Copeland. Harrison House, Incorporated, 1995

Releasing the Mother Goddess by Gail Carr Feldman, Eve Adamson. Alpha, 2003

The Souls of Black Folks by W.E.B. DuBois. Kessinger Publishing, 2004

Spiritual Narratives by Sue E. Houchins. Oxford University Press, 1998

Spiritual Resources in Family Therapy by Froma Walsh. Guilford Press, 1999

Spirituality In Nursing: From Traditional to New Age by Barbara J. Stevens Barnum. Springer Publishing Company, 2003

Success Factors of Young African-American Women At A Historically Black College by Marilyn J. Ross. Praeger/ Greenwood, 2003

10 Good Choices That Empower Black Women's Lives by Grace Cornish. Three Rivers Press, 2001

The Thrill of the Chaste: Finding Fulfillment While Keeping Your Clothes On by Dawn Eden. Thomas Nelson, 2006

The Twelve Gifts of Healing by Charlene A. Costanzo, Alexis Seabrook. Wellness & Lifestyle, an Imprint of Harper-Collins Publishing, 2004

What Mama Couldn't Tell Us About Love: Healing the Emotional Legacy of Slavery, Celebrating Our Light by

Brenda Richardson, Brenda Wade. HarperCollins Publishers, 1999

Women of a New Tribe: A Photographic Celebration of the Black Woman by Jerry Taliferro. Jerry Taliferro Photography, 2007